African Magic

AFRICAN MAGIC

Traditional Ideas that Heal a Continent

HEIDI HOLLAND

VIKING

VIKING

Published by the Penguin Group
27 Wrights Lane, London W8 5TZ, England
Penguin Putnam Inc, 375 Hudson Street, New York, New York 10014, USA
Penguin Books Australia Ltd, Ringwood, Victoria, Australia
Penguin Books Canada Ltd, 10 Alcorn Avenue, Toronto, Ontario, Canada M4V 3B2
Penguin Books (NZ) Ltd, Cnr Rosedale and Airborne Roads, Albany, Auckland, New Zealand
Penguin Books India (P) Ltd, 11 Community Centre, Panchsheel Park, New Delhi – 110 017, India
Penguin Books (South Africa) (Pty) Ltd, 5 Watkins Street, Denver Ext 4, Johannesburg 2094, South Africa

Penguin Books (South Africa) (Pty) Ltd, Registered Offices:
Second Floor, 90 Rivonia Road, Sandton 2196, South Africa

First published by Penguin Books (South Africa) Pty) Ltd, 2001

ISBN 0670 89661 6

Typeset by CJH Design in 11/13.5pt Charter
Cover design: African Icons Graphics Studio
Printed and bound by Interpak Books, KwaZulu-Natal

For

LES and IDELY

my parents

Contents

Preface

I am acutely aware of the complexity and sensitivity of the subject of this book: the traditional belief system of Africa. It seemed, at first, too fraught a subject to investigate on the strength of journalistic curiosity.

Did I have the formal credentials to write about African religion? No. Could I quantify the extent to which Africans subscribe to their traditional beliefs in the twenty-first century? No. Did I have the resources to conduct extensive original research on this vast topic? No. Was there any social merit in investigating the subject? Yes.

In deciding that Africa's traditional belief system was a valid subject for me to research – despite being neither anthropologist nor theologian, nor an African raised with the traditional beliefs of this continent – I spent many hours reading newspaper files of stories written over the years. These files, in the library of Johannesburg's oldest daily newspaper published in English, *The Star*, date back half a century to the 1950s. I found many reports about aspects of traditional beliefs, mainly about murders associated with witchcraft. I found interviews with traditional healers describing the ailments they treat. But I did not find a single account telling me what I wanted to know, which was *why* Africans raised with traditional ideas believe what they believe.

This early research helped to validate my initial premise: that English-speaking people living and working in Africa, like myself, know something about the manifestations of some traditional beliefs. But we have virtually no contextual insight into the fragments of traditional religion which are brought to our attention.

Later, in September 2000, I noted that the South African National Conference on Racism 2000 endorsed the need to teach traditional African beliefs to schoolchildren in all communities, urban as well as rural.

I believe journalists are uniquely placed to extend the boundaries of conventional research (outside the preconceived frameworks that inhibit academia) by seeing things which others cannot see – including the need to demystify important social issues. That was why I embarked in 1986 on my first book, *THE STRUGGLE: A History of the African National Congress*, at a time when the ANC was a banned organisation in South Africa.

I was born in Africa and have lived on this continent all my life. Spoon-fed racism with my daily cornflakes throughout my childhood, I have struggled throughout my adult life to see beyond the diet of prejudice and ignorance. At a personal as well as professional level, looking beyond 'witchdoctor' images of African traditional beliefs over the past four years has made sense of some of the nonsense I absorbed as a white person in Africa.

My main sources of information in compiling this book were anthropological texts. These contain the research of hundreds of scholars working throughout sub-Saharan Africa during the twentieth century. An extensive bibliography appears at the end of this book for readers who might wish to explore aspects of African traditional beliefs more fully.

It is a feature of academic research that anthropology texts are written for informed scholars rather than for ordinary readers. In writing this book, I have assumed the role of translating complicated analysis into accessible conclusions; of extracting comprehensible insights from confusing anthropological terminology. If, in pursuit of clarity, I have offended anthropology, I offer in mitigation my journalistic instinct to increase popular awareness of a subject which contains important knowledge for western-orientated teachers, employers, journalists, development agencies and investors who are trying to increase their understanding of the African continent.

Most of the anthropological research informing this book was conducted over the years by white academics assisted by Africans. This approach has come under fire from post-modernist critics, leaving the study of African anthropology as a whole in a crisis of confidence. I have wherever possible verified the findings of white anthropologists with the written research of African theologians and anthropologists, such as John S Mbiti. In the contemporary stories, I have conducted my own research with English-speaking African informants.

I have confined my research to Africa south of the Sahara because, culturally and historically, North Africa is closer to the Middle East than to the rest of the continent. I have accepted the prevailing view of recent scholarship in this field (Christopher Ejizu, E B Idowu and others) that we can legitimately speak of one African traditional religion as the single, basic philosophy of traditional Africa, although this perspective is disputed by some authorities.

The most contentious issue surrounding this subject is the seemingly unanswerable question: How many Africans are guided by the traditional belief system at the start of the twenty-first century?

Says theologian Alyward Shorter in *Concepts of Social Justice in Traditional Africa*:

> One cannot deny that there are many threads of continuity, linking the past with the present, the old social order with the new, but how important are the elements of discontinuity? One of the assumptions . . . is that traditional concepts survive because they find a new dimension and a new application in the modern situation. Traditional Africa is now history, mainly oral history, but that does not mean to say it can be ignored. On the contrary, to recognise traditional concepts and to understand their workings in the modern Africa, it is first of all necessary to see them as part of a political and social order which no longer exists in its pure form.

This argument, increasingly embraced by development agencies and other benefactors, is one of the reasons I have covered great distances of time and space in this book.

The question of how far traditional Africa coexists with modern Africa remains a difficult one. Is the traditional belief system today a feature of the rural areas but not of the cities of Africa? There are no statistics to prove the influence of traditional beliefs on the contemporary cosmology. But it is not hard to find evidence of traditional beliefs in the cities of Africa – in Soweto, for example, which is the largest urban African settlement in modern South Africa.

Attend a funeral in Soweto – any funeral – and you will see the traditional belief system in action in urbanised society. Very few urbanised Africans in Soweto have middle-class parents: virtually all retain their roots in traditional society. One has only to monitor the mass migration of people from Soweto over public holidays to know how many return regularly to their traditional communities. One has only to go to Soweto over a weekend – any weekend – to see large fenced enclosures of goats being sold as sacrificial animals for rituals concerning ancestor worship.

The majority of modern Africans are intensely religious: that is a readily observable fact from Cape to Cairo. Religion has always infused every aspect of life on the continent to such an extent that it is sometimes difficult to isolate and study it. The traditional belief system is, ultimately, a study of the people themselves in all the intricacies of traditional as well as modern life. As such, it ought to be factored into economics and education because ignorance of African beliefs perpetuates misunderstanding of African problems and responses.

Although religion can be studied in terms of its ceremonies and rituals, the philosophy which informs religious activity – the *why* in people's beliefs – is not as easily discernible. Philosophy of some sort lies behind the thoughts and actions of all people everywhere. To study it in Africa as outsiders involves interpretation of the information before us, and interpretation is never free of subjective judgement. That is why I have chosen a story-telling structure for this book, with relatively little interpretation. The selection of the stories is obviously interpretative in itself, but that cannot be helped.

I have chosen an eclectic approach, offering the reader a variety of ways of interpreting the material. It is by no means an exhaustive treatment, for which I am not equipped. I have presented the general nature of traditional African beliefs through a collection of detailed stories of particular religious experiences. In some chapters, I have provided more descriptive depth than in others to give the characters in the stories a living context. I have attempted to give a sense of the historical whole by covering events that occurred as far back as 1856 and as recently as 2000.

Because traditional beliefs permeate every aspect of African life, there is little distinction between secular and sacred, material and spiritual. Where you meet the African, there you will find his religion: in a field harvesting maize; at a funeral ceremony; in the market place. Far from being confined to a church or mosque once a week on Friday or Sunday, the traditional African's religion embraces his whole environment; his entire time on earth and beyond.

Because traditional African religion is not written in scriptures but is inscribed in people's minds and hearts, as well as in their proverbs and sacred ceremonies, any examination of the subject must observe the individual's religious journey, beginning before birth and continuing long after physical death. That is why I have included Camara Laye's beautiful story, *The Dark Child*, in its entirety: he describes far better than I could have done the intensity with which traditional Africans experience every step of the religious journey.

Although use of the terms 'black' and 'white', to denote an African on the one hand and a person of European descent on the other, is commonplace throughout southern Africa and other societies on the continent, they are politically nuanced terms worldwide. I have therefore referred to Africans and whites, the latter having to date adopted no alternative terminology (such as Euro-African along the lines of the North American model). In the earlier stories, I have used the term colonialist where this is obviously appropriate.

What people do is motivated by what they believe, as surely as what people believe stems from their experiences. In describing this process at various levels, I have had no axe to grind. I am neither an occultist nor a materialist, but simply on the side of common sense. My intention has been to facilitate a better understanding of traditional African beliefs as a means of helping the reader discover more about Africa.

If this book raises more questions than it answers, I hope it might encourage African writers with first-hand insights to educate those of us who sincerely want to learn.

Acknowledgements

I would like to thank Sara Mashele, a traditional healer in South Africa, for opening my mind to the other ways of knowing which inspired this book. She came to the bedside of my late husband George Patrikios, a surgeon who suffered irrevocable brain damage in a motor accident. Neither science nor African magic could help him but my recourse to both in desperate times pointed the way to a fascinating journey of discovery: this book. It also gave me the certain knowledge over the seven years of my husband's terrible suffering that 'Hope springs eternal in the human breast . . .' (Alexander Pope), which is the cry at the heart of the traditional beliefs of Africa.

Respected African anthropologists Professor David Hammond-Tooke of Johannesburg and Bishop Peter Sarpong of the Roman Catholic Church in Kumasi, Ghana – both authors and authorities in the field of traditional African beliefs – kindly examined the manuscript for factual errors.

My editors at Penguin Books, Alison Lowry and Pam Thornley, forced me to re-examine my own beliefs and helped me write a better book. I was often helped during four years of research by Fay Blain and Margaret Northey of the Africana Library at the University of the Witwatersrand.

I thank my sons, Jonah Hull and Niko Patrikios, who are always enthusiastically supportive of my books. I thank my parents for everything. My talented friends – Ruth Rice, Amina Cachalia, Ofeibea Quist-Arcton, Caroline Cullinan, Alby James, Nonie Niesewand, Mary Braid, Lorien Brown, Sue Armstrong, Adele Lucas and Suzanne Brenner – give me enriching perspectives when I am muddled, in writing as in life. Mike Donkin, Peter Goldsmid, Fred Bridgland, Karl Muller, Garth Lucas, Paddy Linehan, Adi Critten and my brother Ted Holland contributed valuable insights to this book. Duncan Clarke gave me the gift of his effortless generosity.

Above all, I am indebted to the many scholars whose painstaking research in the field of African anthropology gave me the concepts of understanding, without which I could not have undertaken this book.

One

Traditional Beliefs of Africa

Belief in the supernatural is considered eccentric in the western world, unless the magical beliefs happen to be your own. As often as not, the person whose superstition prevents him from walking under a ladder is the same one who scorns fear of witchcraft. Roman Catholics, who think nothing of gaining spiritual strength by symbolically eating the body and drinking the blood of Christ, will stare in astonishment at the African who believes he is immunising himself against evil by rubbing lion's fat into his skin.

Most of us know it is impossible to appreciate the inner lives of men and women from foreign cultures without some insight into their spiritual landscapes. Yet teachers, employers and journalists of European descent have engaged with Africans for many, many years without any understanding of the belief system by which they make sense of their moral dilemmas.

African Magic seeks to appreciate the idiom or natural philosophy by which traditional Africa explains the relationship between people and unfortunate events: the dynamics of good versus evil. It is not an exhaustive study but a collection of true stories presented to help non-Africans understand the invisible intelligence – or magic – which informs traditional beliefs on the continent.

In this book *magic* is taken to refer to both divination and herbal treatments with special curative properties. It includes rituals and ceremonies involving material substances such as herbs and animal parts, as well as verbal spells which invoke divine intervention if administered correctly. As a generic term, *magic* refers to all esoteric methods of enquiry and their subsequent interpretation by troubled individuals or their spiritual advisers. As a concept in this book, *magic* is the chief foe of witchcraft.

As in any religion, the understanding of African traditional beliefs rests on three main themes. First, the sacred images such as gods and ancestors which regulate the traditional universe. Second, the rituals and ceremonies by which these sacred images communicate moral patterns into living culture. And third, the earthly representatives of gods and ancestors – traditional healers/diviners/prophets/priests and sacred kings – who are the servants of the community with the role of mediating the sacred to the people through rituals and divination. African witchcraft belongs in this latter category because its influence dominates the esoteric knowledge provided by traditional healers and diviners.

Africa's sacred images are mainly ancestor spirits. Although the majority of Africans worship Christ alongside their traditional beliefs, many do not think of God in the same way as Christians know him. He is the creator, known by many names – Lezer in East Africa, Zambia, upper Congo and Tanzania; Chineka and Oluwa by the Igbo and Yoruba people of Nigeria; Mgwo by the Mende of Sierra Leone. He is a spirit force responsible for all life on earth, including the ancestors, but he is too remote to hear the prayers of ordinary mortals. Dead ancestors, being spirits, communicate with God, mediating between him and humanity. Traditional healers or diviners – the prophets, physicians, psychologists and exorcists of African culture – are people chosen by the ancestors to interpret God's will on earth.

Diviners or traditional healers (the two terms are used interchangeably in this book) are found in virtually every African community, urban as well as rural, and feature prominently in the stories that follow. Their role is to search for esoteric knowledge in order to provide solutions where moral choices have to be made among individuals.

Says anthropologist Phillip M Peek in *African Divination Systems*:

> Much as the classroom and the courtroom are primary sites for the presentation of cultural truths in the United States, so the diviner in other cultures is central to the expression and enactment of his or her cultural truths as they are reviewed in the context of contemporary realities . . . Divination systems do not only reflect other aspects of a culture; they are the means . . . of knowing which underpin and validate all else.

Another anthropologist, Professor E E Evans-Pritchard – whose famous book *Witchcraft, Oracles and Magic Among the Azande* blazed the research trail – explains:

> (Traditional healers) can only be understood when considered together with beliefs in witchcraft, as policemen can only be understood in relation to crime. Just as every policeman is a professional indicator of crime, so is every (traditional healer) a

professional indicator of witchcraft.

All human communities throughout history have been fascinated by the idea of special insights and knowledge gleaned through divination. It has provided both a trusted method of decision-making and a basic source of vital knowledge in Africa for centuries. Any examination of African traditional beliefs in the twenty-first century must therefore question the mocking attitude with which African systems of divination have sometimes been dismissed by mainstream scholarship and journalism alike.

Part of the answer is the westerner's conviction that his own worldview is the only valid one: what he fails to understand is therefore rejected as superstition. Through much of the twentieth century, the standard international academic research handbook, *Notes and Queries on Anthropology*, contained only two brief references to African divination in almost four hundred pages. This is partly why misunderstanding of witchcraft – accorded far more space in the same book – has developed at the expense of understanding the social context in which witchcraft occurs.

Since witchcraft is the most widely known and misunderstood manifestation of African traditional beliefs, *African Magic* looks closely at witchcraft in its social environment to show why the phenomenon continues to represent an essential dynamic in African experience.

Misunderstandings abound in this subject. The written study of African traditional beliefs began in the eighteenth and nineteenth centuries with random and culturally prejudiced accounts of travellers, missionaries and colonialists who tended to portray the diviner 'as a charismatic charlatan coercing others through clever manipulation of esoteric knowledge granted inappropriate worth by a credulous and anxiety-ridden people', says anthropologist Phillip Peek.

By the late nineteenth century, anthropologists from western universities had begun to conduct systematic field research. Their findings were expanded from around 1950 by a growing number of theological and philosophical studies written by Africans, which led to attempts to combine anthropological and historical methods of research.

But despite two centuries of systematic study, cultural prejudices have persisted worldwide. Towards the end of the twentieth century British art historian Lord Kenneth Clark, for example, began his widely acclaimed investigation of western art with a comparison between a Greek statue of Apollo and an African ceremonial mask. The latter, he said, reflected a lower state of 'civilisation' in its religious representation of 'fear and darkness', while the Apollo figure embodied a higher state of 'light and confidence'. This inverted and negative perspective, embodied in terms such as 'non-literate' and 'pre-modern', continues to characterise developing continents such as Africa as the opposite of the western world.

Like all religions, African beliefs – including witchcraft – seek to endorse morality, making people kinder to each other. The witch's most fearsome power in African minds is her ability to harm the people with whom she ought to co-operate: neighbours, friends or relatives. She is the opposite of good – the personification of evil. However, she is neither a devil nor a demented spirit but a human being. Hell is not a mystical *place* in traditional Africa: it is the demonic behaviour of other people.

Unlike the Christian's belief in Satan, little dogma is attached to the African witch. Few African communities believe in a hell for the spirits of evil people after death, nor in a heaven for the good, as Christians do. The evil of witchcraft attacks the living, causing people on earth to suffer and die.

No religion in the world offers a universal logic. If Roman

Catholicism is compatible with reason, so is witchcraft to those who reason differently. Catholicism worships a god who is three in one, divine and human. Both belief systems offer passionate insights into the nature of the supernatural and human experience, fusing these with the rational and critical faculties of their believers.

God is not a being but an invisible power in Africa, whereas ancestor spirits continue to exist near their descendants, appearing to the living in dreams as regular people who eat, drink, smoke and argue. This is why, in many African communities, personal belongings such as blankets and cooking utensils are buried in graves alongside deceased relatives, who will continue to need their practical tools and comforts after death.

Being a Christian or subscribing to other religions in no way conflicts with traditional beliefs, even for those called to the priesthood as diviners. Large numbers of Africans have been Christianised for four generations but have maintained a compound rather than a single belief. Over two thousand offshoots from orthodox Christian churches exist in some of Africa's cities as sects combining Judaeo-Christian and indigenous religions. Christianity struggles to accommodate some of the exotic African forms, particularly witchcraft beliefs, yet it is hardly surprising that African Christians still fear the malevolence of witchcraft, just as Europeans did in similar social circumstances during the Renaissance.

Traditional Africa's view of witchcraft is perhaps best described as an analogy with basic medical science. Just as westerners accept that they are constantly exposed to illness through germs, so many Africans believe there is a continual threat of disease and disaster from persons endowed with wickedness. They do not consider what their world would be like without diviners and healers to combat witchcraft any more than westerners wonder what life would be like without physicians.

As Professor Evans-Pritchard demonstrated among the Azande of the Sudan/Congo, witchcraft beliefs attempt to explain the inexplicable and control the uncontrollable in respect of misfortune and illness.

Belief in witchcraft contends that evil forces in society can be manipulated by specially endowed individuals to the detriment of ordinary people. It holds that every community since the beginning of time has contained people with malevolent intentions, who cause havoc during their lives and whose spirits after death select suitable individuals – witches – to possess and endow with wickedness. Extreme goodness and kindness is also believed to be hereditary. It is handed on by deceased relatives – ancestral spirits – to deserving individuals, namely, traditional healers.

Witchcraft is a theory of causation to which traditional Africans attribute the misfortunes that prove harmful to themselves. It is not considered the sole cause of dangerous phenomena, such as lightning or fire. Everyone knows fire is meant to burn, but it is not supposed to burn *you*. Equally, lightning strikes are a common occurrence, resulting in death only when caused by witchcraft.

Because traditional Africa trusts in the inherent good of worldly existence, destiny is linked to actions. Misfortune is not a matter of chance but is associated with the ire of the ancestor spirits or the evils of witchcraft.

If lightning strikes a rural community in Africa and causes injury, someone is to blame. If a relative dies in a road accident, if a crop unexpectedly fails or a baby contracts a serious illness, the victims believe it was caused by witchcraft – unless there is strong evidence and oracular confirmation to the contrary.

Ancestor spirits who normally protect the family left on earth can withdraw this protection if upset by a living member of the clan. Sickness can result from the wrath of formerly benign forebears, who are ever present and absorbed in the lives of their descendants. They must be appeased continually, especially in troubled times, lest they be angered through neglect and jealousy or slighted by broken religious tenets.

Displeased ancestor spirits usually reveal themselves in dreams. An offending descendant then consults a traditional healer, who prescribes immediate appeasement of the ancestors through ritual ceremonies featuring ancient heirlooms and sacrificial feasts. Family quarrels are the surest way to excite the rage of the ancestors, so keeping peace with everyone at home is a constant preoccupation.

Traditional healers, including herbalists, are the mediators of the spirit world and fulfil a three-fold function: religion, divination and medicine. They keep in touch with the ancestors, ascertaining the cause of misfortune and prescribing remedies; they expose evil-doers and identify witches, providing charms and medicines with mystical properties to ward off evil; and, through the study of plants, they administer herbal extracts in the treatment of disease. The person requiring help goes first to a diviner, who conducts a diagnostic ritual to discover the cause of the complaint. Depending on the outcome, the patient may then be referred to a herbalist for treatment. Many healers combine both functions.

Witchcraft in Africa falls into various categories. A witch is believed to cause harm by casting a spell or cursing someone. A victim of misfortune is often diagnosed as bewitched by a traditional healer, who then identifies the perpetrator of the disaster through a process of divination. In instances of personal rivalry in some African countries, however, an individual who never considered herself a witch may verbally abuse another in a fit of jealousy, by saying something like 'I wish you were dead!' If harm thereafter befalls the person angrily cursed in this way, suspicion of witchcraft may fall on the one who did nothing more than express hatred. So anybody is haplessly capable of committing witchcraft and, if identified as a witch, is under intense pressure to accept responsibility. This is why ordinary people with no supernatural history and no guilt beyond ill-temper sometimes concede guilt when accused of witchcraft.

Another form of witchcraft occurs when someone with a grievance visits a traditional healer or herbalist to obtain substances for the purposes of, say, summoning the lightning bird to strike a person or property. The person buying the magical substances as well as the supplier may then be accused of dealing in witchcraft. This is where the distinction between traditional healers and witches becomes blurred.

Other types of witches, invariably women, knowingly rise naked from their beds during the night and blow a magic substance kept in an animal horn in the direction of the person who is to be harmed or killed. In some parts of Africa, she is believed to remain bodily in her bed with only her spirit emerging to perform the wicked deed. Some of these women make use of zombies – the living dead – who are resurrected from graves and made to work for the witches under cover of darkness. Some witches assign familiars to conduct their evil deeds. These agents are either animals – the lightning bird, owl, snake or wildcat, kept by witches as pets – or monsters like the *thokoloshe* of southern Africa.

Once indoctrinated into a belief system from early childhood, the faith often runs too deep for critical analysis, especially in the absence of scientific education. African nurses often choose traditional rather than modern medicine for treatment of their own illnesses, even though they are medically trained and continually watch patients recover through scientific drug therapy. They do not perceive the contradiction because they have no theoretical interest in the subject, traditional remedies being integral to their view of illness and misfortune. They also know that the recovered African patient will in most cases have consulted a traditional healer somewhere along the line, so that his recovery may be a combination of science and traditional remedies.

It is widely accepted throughout Africa that everyone runs the risk of being harmed by a witch: sooner or later, the evil is likely to get you. You arm yourself with protective medicine, hoping this will ward off danger but knowing that it sometimes fails. When 'infected', you have recourse to a traditional healer's remedies both to counter the spells and curses and to renew protective measures. And sometimes, if desperately ill, you may end up in a hospital being treated and cured by modern medicine, often realising that the gravity of your illness has been aggravated by the traditional healer's remedies.

The social purpose of witchcraft accusations is to apportion blame for misfortune and to ensure that each member of a community has an equal share in its prosperity – an anthropological concept known as The Image of Limited Good. Whether accusations are precipitated by someone dying or harm befalling a group through illness, damaged property or failed crops, the harmony of the community is disturbed and must be restored. If the disturbance cannot be ascribed to ancestor spirits, a witch must be found.

Although expressed in different ways, the Image of Limited Good prevails throughout Africa and lies at the heart of witchcraft accusations. It is the belief that the pie is limited and one person's success is always at the expense of another's. If an individual prospers beyond the expectations of the others in his community, the successful one may be labelled a witch because he is believed to have augmented personal progress via witchcraft and to have impoverished others in the process. (Victims of witchcraft are often relatively prosperous individuals.)

This notion breeds constant envy in traditional communities. Africans believe the witch's damaging hatred comes from her remorseless jealousy of others. And ordinary people are assumed to run a greater risk of being attacked by witchcraft if they become more prosperous than their neighbours because they are inviting not only the jealousy of the village but also of the witch.

Not all misdemeanours are linked to witchcraft. It is not suspected in cases of ordinary theft, for example. A thief steals only in order to further his own ends, not because he has a grudge against anyone. Witchcraft is suspected only where the theft is thought to arise from jealousy.

Interestingly, no matter how embittered Africans become towards white employers or foes, they do not allege witchcraft in their case. This is partly because African magic is considered powerless in an alien environment: witches are invariably insiders who harm their neighbours. But it is also because witchcraft is a theory of power as well as a theory of evil. In central and southern Africa, it is often seen as the power of the poorest members of society: the witch is a deprived individual driven by jealousy to harm those more fortunate. Most whites, being more powerful than the majority of Africans, are unlikely to envy Africans and are therefore antithetical to the concept of witchcraft.

Traditional healers loathe the term *witchdoctor*, still used by conservative whites, because it has been mocked by settlers for centuries and implies that the healer is a witch. While he does diagnose and 'treat' witchcraft, like a doctor, the traditional healer is primarily engaged in curative magic –

with some exceptions.

Sometimes traditional healers (particularly herbalists) engage in medicine murders, the grisly crimes committed when human body parts are required for particularly powerful magic. Such healers, thought by some to be possessed by evil spirits and by others to be charlatans, are indistinguishable from witches.

Because the corpses of victims mutilated in pursuit of body parts are seldom buried but usually thrown into rivers, the incidence of medicine murders goes largely unreported. Judging from court records of the rare cases that have been prosecuted, the killers are generally hired criminals who are paid large sums by wealthy individuals for breasts, brains or genitals. The herbalist co-ordinates the crime, identifying the body parts required as well as the type of victim whose flesh will yield the best results.

Medicine murders occur because many Africans believe success in business, politics or scholastic endeavour is achieved through the supernatural and not the individual's own efforts. Human hands, ears, noses, lips and eyes – especially from young, virile and preferably living victims – are thought to provide personal success by securing advantages from the spirit world. A hand may be built into the foundations of a new shop to ensure good trading; a brew of human parts buried in a field to guarantee a good harvest. Eyes symbolise clarity of judgement; blood enhances vitality. The supernatural power sought in a medicine murder is believed to be awakened by the victim's screams.

Another departure in some African societies from the general truth that traditional healers or herbalists set out to perform only curative medicine is the belief that a spiritually endowed individual may destroy or inflict serious harm on others if, in so doing, the healer is performing a just act. This is the traditional healer through whose spirit justice is restored. If someone in the community wrongs another – for example, by stealing valuables, refusing to pay a debt or committing adultery – and the victim is unable to obtain redress through legal channels, he can seek a medium with the power to punish the guilty party by inflicting madness, illness or death on successive family members. The vengeful attacks persist until their cause is recognised and blame accepted by the offending family.

Traditional healers are taught, initially by their human mentors while qualifying as diviners or herbalists and later by their guiding ancestor spirits, where to find the particular herbs and potions which will cure an illness, restore a husband's love or determine the sex of a baby. The witch has an equally wide herbal knowledge but only of magic with dangerous propensities, revealed to her through evil spirits.

Acquiring herbal expertise is a protracted vocation: traditional healers experiment lifelong with plants and animal parts to achieve remedies they sometimes claim to have been given by their ancestors in dreams. Often, there is an empirical rather than a mystical basis to these cures, hence the interest of the international pharmaceutical industry in some traditional African remedies.

There are medicines for every complaint and aspiration, either dug from fields and forests by individual spiritual specialists to fulfil prescriptions for their own clients, or purchased from herbalists' shops in the cities of Africa. They include rare lizard fat, snake skin, sunburnt beetles and spiders, lion lard, dried crocodile liver and baboon testicles, although most are of botanical origin.

Many of the remedies might be termed sympathetic magic: to ensure a good journey, the prescription is made from a root that sends out runners and therefore knows its way. Belief that qualities can be transferred means that a cream made from the beautifully sleek skin of the python will make the hide of cattle gleam, or lion's fat smeared on the arms and legs of a soldier will make him feared by his enemies. To give a person security, the herbalist might administer a portion of the body of the steadfast tortoise; for swiftness, the sinew of a hare.

When a wife suspects her husband is turning to another woman, she buys a tasteless powder and adds it to his food in the belief that his affection for her will be restored. If a woman is unable to conceive a child, she inhales a substance that promotes fertility. A sure seller is a powder made from lion paws and bought by the mothers of timid children to ward off bullying at school.

Next to lion parts with courageous properties, crocodiles are highly prized by herbalists. Considered a mighty and magical animal, the crocodile has teeth which renew themselves, he feeds on living flesh, and his hide can deflect bullets.

While it is obvious today to western minds that the malevolence of witchcraft lies in the belief rather than any real power, the same belief prevailed in many other cultures worldwide prior to the spread of scientific knowledge, and is still rife in continents like South America. The last witch was burnt in England in 1722, but schoolchildren all over the world continue to study Shakespeare's witches, those most famous of cackling hags with whiskery jaws and Halloween hats, stirring hellish brews of toads and fingernails.

Witchcraft beliefs offer a kind of catharsis to assuage fear, the need for revenge, feelings of jealousy in the face of disparity of circumstances, and the mystery of inexplicable misfortune. They provide society with scapegoats, a metaphor literally evoked in a Zimbabwean ceremony performed to cleanse a witch of her evil: she transfers her malign spirit to a black goat and chases it far away.

Many more women than men are accused of witchcraft today, although it seems to have been the other way around in some African countries in the past. This may reflect gender conflict as a result of the gradual enhancement of women's status in urban life. Witch hunts in rural areas often occur during December and are usually led by men who, returning on holiday to their villages after working long months in demeaning jobs in the city, are eager to take charge.

Witch hunts sometimes focus on grand conspiracies, such as crop failure seen as intent to starve the community, but more often on humble personal struggles that are viewed as abnormal. In some African communities, if a woman has difficulty delivering her child or if her baby refuses to suckle, she may be suspected of having had sex with a witch's familiar. Since it is believed that her labour will proceed normally once she confesses, the tormented mother is only too eager to admit to dreaming of visiting graves and devouring the flesh of the dead. Such confessions apparently occur frequently and attest to the reality of witchcraft, giving it the illusion of fact.

Nobody sees a witch going about her wicked deeds. The witch sees you, but is herself invisible. Her familiars are hidden or move about in disguise. The rare individual who sees a witch immediately suffers amnesia. And so the key assumptions of witchcraft defy critical scrutiny. Only circumstantial evidence and confessions are left to confirm the reality of the belief.

In general, all situations that heighten social tension may lead to accusations of witchcraft, most often where there is close contact between people. The more intimate the contact, the greater the risk, except where there is a close blood relationship (a rule sometimes ignored in societies in rapid transition).

Death and sickness, especially of babies, are the most common events precipitating witchcraft accusations. Infant mortality is still so high in Africa that a constant fear exists in the minds of parents that some evil magic will take away their children.

Apart from struggling to comprehend the ongoing high mortality and morbidity confronting people all over Africa, those whose earliest memories feature witchcraft beliefs are inclined to attribute their personal failures as well as their misfortunes to supernatural practice.

Court records indicate that young adults rarely accuse others of witchcraft (although exceptions have occurred throughout the continent during civil and colonial wars). The allegations are usually made by people who have reached the stage in life when they have either failed to achieve their ambitions or realised that there are insurmountable obstacles to be overcome if their desires are to be realised. It is then that they tend to blame others. A death, illness or disappointment gives rise to suspicions directed towards a particular individual, who is then accused of thwarting the other's success.

There is almost always an existing state of tension between the accused and the complainant. Harsh words may have been exchanged, there may have been a clash of temperaments or the accused may have shown indifference to the misfortune of the complainant. The tension may have gone on for some time without repercussion. But once something unpleasant happens, the complainant wonders who might wish him harm and finds his mind constantly brooding on the accused, who becomes his suspect. As often as not, the accused is a person who has aroused the jealousy of the complainant.

This is why traditional African cultures consider it very important never to boast or discuss success, never to express undue anger, and never to seem unsympathetic to another's misfortune. Wherever there is friction or inequality, there exists the seed for an accusation of witchcraft. All that is required is a belief in African magic, and the rest follows.

A relative who fails to attend a burial service, for example, arouses deep suspicion of having caused the death and runs the risk of witchcraft accusation. All relations are expected to hasten to the place of death as soon as they hear the news so as to share the sorrow of the family. One who arrives a week later might be held responsible for the death. It is also expected that those living in a village when a relative is dying should not leave their homes for any reason whatsoever, least of all to return to work.

Some anthropologists who have studied the personalities not only of the ones accused of being witches but also of those who accuse, suggest marked similarities between witches and their victims. According to anthropologist R Godfrey Lienhardt, '. . . the individual who thinks he is hated easily hates; the person who sees others as bearing malice towards him is one who himself feels malice'.

In different parts of Africa, certain physical or personality characteristics are especially likely to be associated with witches. The Lugbara people who occupy the Congo-Nile divide are suspicious of the person whose face is grey and drawn and who walks about at night, and the one who tends to sit and eat alone. They also distrust people who are over-friendly. The stereotypical witch has an unhappy disposition, wears a sullen expression and rarely laughs. A person who is selfish and miserly runs the risk of being linked to witchcraft. The Wolof clan of the western Sudan suspect the one who is shy and furtive. There is widespread anxiety about eccentric and physically handicapped Africans, as well as those who live alone or are childless. The Dinka of southern Sudan believe witchcraft accusations are avoided if a person fosters favourable qualities such as plumpness, good hair, graceful movements, chivalry and generosity.

Where witchcraft practice is suspected, there are strict procedures for accusation. The family consults a traditional healer to learn the reason for the misfortune which has befallen them. The healer may fail to confirm a witch's involvement, and there the matter will rest. But once the healer names a witch, invariably someone living in the same village as the victim, the family declares its accusation by leaving a small heap of ash or some other token in the doorway of the accused's house during the night. When the suspect awakes and acknowledges the accusation, often amid strenuous protests, he or she goes to see the headman who arranges a trial by ordeal.

A specialist in this field officiates – usually a traditional healer. Roots and herbs are boiled up in a brew which is drunk by the accused in front of the assembled community. If the suspect vomits, she is declared innocent in some ceremonies. If found guilty by various tests, she may confess and be spared following suitable rituals. Or, if still protesting her innocence, she may be killed in a ceremony conducted at sunrise, or beaten and driven away like a wild animal.

Such trials by ordeal occur in most but not all African societies. In some ceremonies, when the witch beseeches the spirits to accept her confession, the traditional healer takes a white chicken, slits its throat, and throws the bird into the centre of the gathering. Fluttering and jerking, the fowl is studied in its death throes to establish if it dies on its back with its feet in the air, signalling a cure. If it lies in any other position, the witch's confession is deemed incomplete. As many as a dozen chickens may be sacrificed before one of them dies in the correct position.

Some traditional healers exorcise evil from possessed individuals by absorbing the demon spirit into their own bodies. One of the most respected living diviners in Africa is a majestic, six-foot-two Namibian woman named Katjambia. The daughter of a famous chief of the nomadic Himba, she travels around the region healing bewitched pastoralists. To the rhythm of a drum and a calabash rattle, she induces her patient into a state of trance. Once the possessing spirit has become agitated, Katjambia is able to identify the curse causing the illness, which is believed to be carried by a black dove from neighbouring Angola. Having made a diagnosis, Katjambia takes possession of the spirit and exorcises it from herself, at which moment a celestial light is said to flash from her body.

The mythology of African witchcraft is as vivid as the ancient legends of Greece and medieval Germany. Because witches inherit their supernatural powers, the Sotho witch-parent in South Africa is said to throw each of her new-born babies against the wall of the hut to test if it has inherited the role. The infant that clings to the wall like a bat is the one who will be carefully nurtured in the skills of witchcraft, beginning with charmed milk suckled from the possessed mother's breast.

Although African healers increasingly refer their clients to hospitals and clinics when their traditional remedies prove futile, patients sometimes resist hospitalisation. This is partly because witches are said to use bodily exuviae, such as nail and hair clippings, urine or stool samples, to harm their victims. People who believe in witchcraft fear their excreta might get into dangerous hands while they are in hospital.

Modern doctors who decry traditional healers most vociferously are the ones who know that critically ill patients could have been saved had they not wasted valuable time consulting their own healers. Doctors treating a common form of septicaemia, the result of enemas made from crushed beetles, accuse African healers of criminal activity because the highly acidic insects burn the lining of the intestine, often causing death.

Not surprisingly, western medicine has maintained a sceptical distance from traditional healers, although some doctors – aware that the practice of psychiatry only became a recognised science in the twentieth century, and aware of international research showing that forty per cent of illnesses originate in psychological disorders – realise they can learn from a healing tradition which has prevailed in Africa for thousands of years.

Western civilisation, being technology and concept orientated, relies largely on logical explanations, while Africans live closer to the world of the unconscious and rely on their intuition and feelings; on images or dreams rather than concepts. Chance, an abstract idea based on the acceptance of chaotic happenings, can have no place in a worldview founded on belief in the unity and order of human experience. A scientifically explicable though unusual occurrence like the birth of twins, for example, is viewed with dismay in some traditional African cultures: a witch must have cursed the mother. (In other communities, including the Fon people of Benin, twins are considered sacred and are cherished above all children.)

Apart from its effects on the practice of medicine, belief in witchcraft exerts a unique influence on society. It promotes polite behaviour, serving as a warning against hostile words and deeds. People are constantly reminded not to offend others because they might turn out to be witches. Since enmity is an expression of witchcraft, it should not be voiced openly for fear of accusations of sorcery. A sort of negative morality results: it is better not to make enemies because hatred is the mainspring of witchcraft.

On the one hand, the characteristics of those accused of witchcraft are actively discouraged by society in order to avoid the evil label, but, at the other extreme, the person who achieves obvious wealth and success or is devoted to the pleasures of life is liable to be associated with witchcraft. People raised in traditional society have therefore been taught for generations to be pleasant and unassuming and to resist the desire to stand out from the crowd. Any examination of the effects of witchcraft beliefs, particularly those factors contributing to lack of material progress in Africa, needs to consider whether these beliefs are so intimately woven into everyday thinking that they endorse conformity to the detriment of change.

The modern working mothers of Africa, whose progressive influence ought to be profoundly imprinted on the young, are mainly employed in cities as domestic workers, especially in countries with large and wealthy settler populations like South Africa. In one of the most damaging systemic abuses ever to have blighted the continent, no accommodation is provided in the workplace for their families. Many of the children of urbanised parents have to be sent back to the rural areas to be raised by grandmothers in village homes characterised by unwavering faith in witchcraft. They return to the cities as young adults, barely educated, complete with the belief system of a generation ago.

As an ongoing theory of causation and a system of moral philosophy, witchcraft will continue to exert its influence on Africa's development for many years to come because of the view that the more you have, the more likely you are to attract a witch's envy. This is the antithesis of the western parental gospel: achieve scholastically, compete relentlessly and shine individually. If it is true that belief in witchcraft has promoted mediocrity by dampening the individual's desire for material gain, it must be among the causes of inadequate economic progress in Africa.

But World Bank perspectives are not what this book is about. There are few people anywhere on earth who worship at the shrines of science and money alone. The beginning of the twenty-first century has seen the exploration of New Age spiritual forms on a dramatic scale all over the world, with many technological triumphs being damned as mere illusions of progress. What has not changed even in minds and hearts distracted by shiny things is the clash of good and evil, which needs no argument in a continent shattered by tyranny and greed.

We can lurk behind astringently scientific terms, snigger with the sceptic, admire the materialist. But there will always be two vital principles to challenge the world – good and evil. Most of us pray to a god, or whatever symbolises goodness, when we are lonely and afraid.

Whether we stare in disbelief at the New Age diviner reading tarot cards in her Parisian drawing room or at the ghoulish entrails with which the Venda healer is busy in his dark mountain cave, they represent distinctions without differences in the ancient quest to identify right from wrong, good from evil.

That is what this book is about: the Eternal Conflict as Africans know it.

Two

Prophets and Prophecies

African prophets inspire popular religious movements on the continent. Unlike traditional healers, who are the spiritual consultants serving society, prophets communicate divine messages directly to their followers rather than through symbolic mediums.

Often the sources of religious as well as political change, prophets are powerful leaders with vast innovative scope. Their influence is so great that they occasionally subvert bona fide religious movements for personal gain: a messianic or millenarian movement might then become an apocalyptic cult with dire consequences. Such a tragedy befell followers of the Restoration of the Ten Commandments of God cult in Uganda at the dawn of the twenty-first century when 470 of its members apparently committed mass suicide in March 2000.

The benign influence a great African prophet named Chikanga exerted over the lives of millions of people in four countries began nearly half a century ago when his reputation first spread from Malawi to Tanzania, Zambia to Zimbabwe. Most of those who sought his magic are no longer alive to describe his methods of divination but his legend is undiminished.

He was born Lighton Chunda, a Henga man from Ihete village in the south Rumpi hills of northern Malawi. Well educated, with seven years of primary schooling, and a member of the Church of Central Africa Presbyterian, he was otherwise a typical African peasant of the Fifties.

He became ill in 1956 and consulted a traditional healer, who treated him for symptoms thought to signal his calling by the ancestor spirits to become a diviner. When he recovered, he adopted the name Chikanga, meaning courage, and began to practise his new vocation, specialising both in curing the illness from which he had suffered and revealing the identities of witches.

He was suspended from the Presbyterian Church for believing in witchcraft but his fame had by then spread beyond the borders of his own country. Known as 'the patient prophet with the whispery voice', he seemed unstoppable by 1961, when he was attracting large numbers of people from the areas of Tanzania nearest the lake shore, particularly the Nyasa clan. The following year, thousands of disciples from Mufindi in the southern Uhehe region of Tanzania joined the crowds of troubled people seeking his counsel. By 1964, most Tanzanians knew somebody who had benefited from Chikanga's extraordinary spiritual insights, and his reputation had meanwhile spread into northern Zambia and Zimbabwe.

The Tanzanian people's strongest spirit medium prior to

Chikanga, dating back to the German conquest, was an invisible force called Chansi which lived in a rock in the Ulanga valley. The relatively short journey to consult Chansi had always been a major undertaking for impoverished Tanzanians, yet the advent of Chikanga, a new healer with a proven record, attracted an immediate clientele who began crossing the border in droves, even when the journey to Malawi to consult him cost up to a year's cash income.

Chikanga was believed to exert extraordinary power over witchcraft. It was said that suspected witches who resisted his summonses were driven to see him by abnormal means, such as on bicycles propelled magically through the air. Legend recalls a man who, attempting to get off a bus bound for Chikanga, was stricken with such intense pain that he pleaded to be allowed back on board. Another man allegedly gave birth to a bewitched baby in similar circumstances. A woman healer, who was called by Chikanga but refused to go, was said to have dropped dead for no apparent reason.

Although Chikanga inherited his divination powers in the traditional way, manifested by an illness nearly a decade earlier, the story of his mysticism became embellished. According to the unpublished diary of Anglican missionary L Hurst, he was reputed to have gone to South Africa in search of work, quarrelled tragically with his brother and become ill as a result, died and gone to his grave, and then miraculously risen from the dead. When he arose, the legend claimed, he had acquired a mission from God: to cleanse Africa of witchcraft – a formidable undertaking, all agreed, but one which was accepted as the only hope of reducing sickness and death on the continent.

Thus Chikanga became the leader of one of the witch cleansing cults that occur in fairly regular cycles every ten years or so in some rural regions of Africa, apparently as a symbolic attempt to reorder society by creating new forms of social consciousness. Such cults are thought by anthropologists to arise when communities – rather than individuals – feel the need to protect themselves against witchcraft by neutralising the power of the witch through collective attempts to identify those with evil powers.

One of the characteristics of African witch cleansing cults is their ability to adapt ritual and ideology across ethnic boundaries. Neither language, custom nor, in some cases, lingering hostilities deter the proselytising process once it gets under way.

At the time when Chikanga's influence was sweeping through central Africa, another witch-hunter was capturing the imagination of the Kenyan nation. Nicknamed Kajiwe, meaning 'uncrushable', he achieved heroic status by promising to eradicate witchcraft among the Mijikenda people. Many compared his popularity to that of Alice Lenshina's prophetic movement in Zambia a few years earlier, a phenomenon repeated in 1987 by namesake Alice Lakwena in Uganda, where many devotees lost their lives in clashes with government forces.

Unlike the Ugandan leadership's fear of Alice Lakwena's popularity, which provoked armed repression, the Kenyan authorities hoped the eradication of witchcraft might spur development. They speculated that the economic tardiness of the Mijikenda was the result of fear that individuals would be struck down by jealous neighbours and relatives by the devices of witchcraft if they progressed beyond their peers in farming, trade or education.

While it is unclear whether the witch cleansing cult led by Chikanga first arose from Christian-influenced popular indignation against witchcraft or through his prophecies, the two at some stage merged. Proclaiming a new enlightened age free of pain, illness, violence, hunger and hardship, Chikanga's disciples went from village to village holding secret negotiations with headmen, who were invariably eager to co-operate: anything less than enthusiasm for a witch cleansing initiative might be construed as covert allegiance, especially if surrounding communities had already agreed to support regeneration rituals.

The initial propaganda drive was followed by cleansing procedures, beginning with witch detection that involved unconventional methods of discovery rather than traditional forms of divination. Hand mirrors were a favoured device; cult representatives peered into them at the reflections of villagers filing past behind them, picking out those against whom witchcraft accusations might be made by the community.

There followed the customary trial by ordeal. Suspected witches, longing to be accepted back into their communities as quickly as possible, usually confessed to acts which left no doubt about their guilt. Sena, Chewa and Lomwe suspects from various parts of Malawi readily admitted to raiding graves in the dead of night in order to cut human flesh from recently buried corpses. When the cult spread into Tanzania, Fipa women claimed to have devoured their own children; Shona from Zimbabwe described the removal of internal organs from live, screaming victims. The confessions endorsed the cult, providing proof of its effectiveness in the campaign to flush out witches.

It is unclear whether or not all the ritual steps in the witch cleansing drama common to many African societies were followed in Chikanga's movement. Usually, the last act calls for doses of protective medicine to be given to the entire community. Thereafter, assured that witchcraft is finally vanquished, the community forgives the self-confessed witches as if their heinous sins had never existed. The past is forgotten and everyone looks forward to a better tomorrow.

Witch cleansing cults are particularly puzzling because they are ambiguous both in motivation and effect. They seem to aim at reinforcing harmony and unity in traditional communities. But, by spreading across national and ethnic boundaries, they are also radical, simultaneously encouraging new social divisions. Acolytes of a witch hunting cult, as well as its leader, often achieve social power on a scale that threatens politicians, who fear the cult's innovative potential to create new social institutions – although they seldom transcend their symbolism.

Not all African societies experience witch cleansing movements. Neither the Kikuyu of Kenya nor the Bantu of South Africa, both of whom continue to believe in witchcraft as an explanation for misfortune, have been affected by such cults. Perhaps this is because Kenya and South Africa have been acutely affected by political changes involving social and economic reforms. Witch cleansing cults tend to arise in those parts of the continent that are remote from reformative processes such as the influence of political parties.

* * *

John Kahamele first heard about the great healer Chikanga after being stricken for some time with a growth that suddenly appeared on his left thigh during the winter of 1961. He ignored the tumour until it began to rub against his other thigh, making walking difficult.

Then he consulted a herbalist in a village near his home in Mwanza, southern Malawi, waddling awkwardly with his legs wide apart on a journey which should have taken an hour but lasted most of the day. Being a large man, his thighs rubbed together no matter how hard he tried to keep them apart. By the time he got home, his eyes streaming with tears of frustration and pain, the growth had rubbed raw and he yelped angrily as his wife applied the herbalist's powder.

The growth did not shrink as the herbalist had predicted: if anything, it grew. Tired of sitting outside his hut day after day because moving around was so painful, he decided to make a second, much longer, journey to Limbe Hospital. This time, a friend accompanied him. His wife made a special cushion to strap between his thighs but it slid down his legs constantly and his back eventually ached so badly at having to bend down and pull the cushion up that he abandoned it on the roadside.

They arrived at the hospital late in the afternoon to be informed that John could not be examined or even admitted until the next morning. It was a cold night in June. As the sky turned violet and the surrounding blue gums rose up to the moon, the two men huddled together on a wooden bench, hungry and thirsty. Sleeping fitfully on his friend's shoulder, John had a dream in which he saw someone creeping up to his hospital bed to steal something from him – perhaps a snip of hair from his head to use in witchcraft.

He and his friend discussed the matter and John decided not to risk admission to the hospital. When dawn broke, he limped back to the road, helped by his friend and supporting himself on a broomstick. They hadn't been walking long when they heard the hum of an approaching vehicle. To their surprise, a lorry drew up in a swirl of dust and the driver leaned out of his cab and offered them a ride.

It was the lorry driver who told John about the extraordinary prophet Chikanga. Once they were back in their village, John and his friend decided to go in search of the famous priest, who was thought to be healing and preaching somewhere in the north of Malawi not far from Mbamba Bay. Their headman offered to make enquiries on their behalf and, several months later, they were told to go to Rumpi, close to the Zambian border. Very early one morning, the two men set off to catch a bus.

They travelled for two days, with long waits between buses when they bought mugs of tepid water and bananas from vendors at the roadside. Although it was winter, the pitiless sun made everything hard and glaring during the day, while they froze at night. They began to wish that they had never left home.

When they reached Rumpi they found long lines of people, many of them Malawians, as well as some Fipa and Hehe people from Tanzania who spoke a language they did not understand. They had all been waiting patiently for days for transport to Chikanga's village. John decided to remain seated inside the bus while his friend walked up and down the aisle to stretch his legs. Fortunately for them, the same bus was going to Njakwa and the driver did not notice them in the back, so they went on without delay. They waited there for hours for their last bus, finding seats only in the early hours of the morning.

Chikanga's village, also called Chikanga, consisted of several long, thatched houses where visitors slept, and the diviner's own round hut where he received a steady stream of people from early morning until late at night. There were sleeping bodies all over the floors of the dormitories and it was only at daybreak, when some of them rose to cook food on the fires that were burning outside, that John and his friend found enough space to lie down.

When he awoke in the middle of the morning, John reported to an orderly seated on a beer crate outside the door of the hut. He took down John's details and explained how Chikanga worked.

Each morning the prophet's chief aide, a former policeman

called Pilatu, blew a whistle to assemble the pilgrims and announce a date. This was the signal for people who had arrived in the village on that date, usually around a week earlier, to line up to see Chikanga. Those whose arrival date was not announced returned to the shady places where they had been discussing one another's problems, to sit out another day.

Those whose time had finally come to consult Chikanga stood in the sun in long lines that stretched far beyond the huts. One of the queues was a double line of individuals who had been called to the village by Chikanga to confess their misdeeds, standing next to the person they had allegedly harmed. The other queues were single lines of people waiting for Chikanga to determine the cause of their problems.

They filed slowly into Chikanga's hut. Those who had been suspected of witchcraft but absolved of their evil deeds by Chikanga the previous day stood singing behind the sofa where the healer lay propped up on cushions, his eyes half-open as though he were deeply exhausted or in a trance. He was not yet forty, wore ordinary clothes with no spiritual adornments, was unshaven, and had unkempt hair and hands that were never still.

When John's turn came to enter the hallowed hut, he was told by the departing pilgrim to go straight to the sofa and kneel down in front of Chikanga. The diviner peered at him briefly and then clasped John's shirt at the collar, drawing him towards him. After hearing a brief description of John's illness, Chikanga announced that he was neither a witch nor a sorcerer and told him to report to Pilatu to have scarifications cut into his feet, thumbs, cheeks and neck, into which magical herbs would be rubbed before he returned to Chikanga two days hence for a verdict on the cause of his misfortune.

It was dark when John walked away from Chikanga's

rondavel. He felt dazed from the inspiring audience as well as his intense hunger. The second whistle of the day sounded, a signal for those still waiting in line to collect twigs and a log of wood to place on the fire in the centre of Chikanga's hut.

John's friend had bought tomatoes from an old woman who, like so many others carrying baskets loaded with fresh produce, lived in a neighbouring village and traded briskly with the people waiting to consult Chikanga. The two men sat down to eat the tomatoes with chunks of stale bread. Discussing Chikanga's attitude to the multitudes who travelled great distances for his help, they agreed the prophet's insistence on low prices for food sold in his village was the only reason they could afford to eat at all, and it was only because Chikanga himself charged no fees that they could be there to consult him in the first place. Although cold and still hungry, they reassured each other of their good fortune in obtaining the counsel of so famous a healer.

Another day passed, during which they discussed their problems, not least the looming matter of feeding themselves without money while awaiting prophecies that might come in instalments over several weeks. Then they heard that Pilatu could speed up the process for those with no means of survival. John queued for two hours to appeal to Pilatu, who agreed that Chikanga would issue his pronouncements the following day in one session.

The whole of the next day John stood in line after the first whistle. At sundown, he finally stepped into Chikanga's hut and knelt before the great healer, who again seized his shirt at the collar, drawing their faces close together.

Chikanga began to describe a number of family deaths. John nodded vigorously throughout the meeting because everything the healer said was true, including the actual names of people, some of them relatives, who had caused his family harm over the years. When Chikanga described his father's sister's gory death by hitherto unidentified killers and named the villains, John was so amazed that he gaped at Chikanga, too stunned for speech.

Chikanga waited patiently for his client to collect his thoughts. John eventually exclaimed that the ones he had named were the dead woman's nephews. Chikanga nodded sympathetically, explaining that the young men had acted on the instructions of a bogus diviner, killing their aunt in exactly the macabre way he had prescribed. 'Was she a witch?' asked John. Chikanga shook his head but did not elaborate.

Sceptics in the queue where those accused of witchcraft waited had speculated that the reason Chikanga was so accurate was because he had emissaries planted among them; they listened to family histories and secretly informed the prophet. But it was now obvious to John that there were far too many people seeing Chikanga every day for this to be so, especially in view of the prophet's accuracy, down to the smallest detail, in his own case. For example, Chikanga described the birthmark on the face of one of his deceased uncles, which John had himself forgotten until reminded of it.

Chikanga then named two traditional healers who had treated John and his relatives in the past, implying that they had been involved in some of the deaths. John asked questions which the healer answered readily, and with each answer John's faith in Chikanga's powers grew. Finally, Chikanga addressed the matter of John's physical complaint, saying that the growth on his leg was the result of poor relations with one of his brothers-in-law, a subject not properly identified by the traditional healer John had originally consulted. The man in question was one of the two healers already identified by Chikanga as responsible for the problems in John's life.

Chikanga told John he would summon the two men who had claimed to be healers and shave them, a common process whereby a series of small cuts are made in the temples, on the cheeks, the throat and hands, through which evil forces in the body escape.

When the audience with Chikanga was over, John gave Pilatu the names of the bogus healers. Pilatu's clerk wrote out two summonses in English, addressing them to the headmen who governed the individuals concerned and requesting urgent delivery of the 'very witching' pair. The letters were endorsed with Chikanga's rubber stamp and John was told to collect them the following day after Chikanga had added his signature.

The clerk's instructions contradicted Pilatu's assurance that John would be free to go home immediately after the consultation with Chikanga. But the clerk would not budge and Pilatu had by that time moved away to hear the pleas of another long line of pilgrims. Feeling faint with hunger, John again lined up to speak to Pilatu and remind him of their desperate circumstances.

'We will die before we reach our village,' John told the stern-faced Pilatu when he finally reached the head of the queue. Pilatu nodded and disappeared, returning a short while later with the signed summonses.

The two men queued again to begin their journey home in an old Land Rover owned by an entrepreneur who was reputed to have made a fortune transporting Chikanga's followers. By the time they climbed inside, it was dark and the passengers were too tired to speak.

John managed to find a seat but there was no space among

the passengers huddled on the floor to raise his feet or press them down against the impact of the rough road. His wound throbbed and his back ached. Staring into the darkness, he had a confused recollection of dotted hills on a wide plain, a glimpse of an expanse of water, groups of straight trees, a few thatched huts.

Early in the morning, they transferred to a bus which crawled along the dusty red road, stopping frequently for the driver to pour water into the smoking, hissing radiator. Once, when the bus stopped for so long that it seemed to be going no further that day, John and his friend got out and walked around the tiny halt called Letter Boxi, lined with Indian stores on the verandas of which African tailors sat at treadle sewing machines surrounded by gaudy, flapping fabric.

They managed to beg a banana from a woman who, when she heard of their successful ten-day mission to Chikanga, said she would soon be making the same journey and hoped to encounter kindness along the way. John urged her to take ample food, warning that some pilgrims had to spend over a month completing the divination process. She said there were people who complained about the expense of visiting Chikanga, to which John replied indignantly that it was those providing transport who were making the money, not Chikanga.

* * *

A number of initially sceptical white people met Chikanga and were impressed by him. A road construction engineer from Tanzania was advised to consult Chikanga about his poor relations with the labourers working under him. A few white doctors regularly sent patients with psychological problems to him, and Chikanga sometimes recommended western medicine to his own clients.

Although he was watched closely by the district commissioner of the Rumpi region, no cause was ever found to prosecute Chikanga since he neither charged fees for his services nor caused unrest by naming witches. Some of his acolytes did identify witches but there was scant evidence to link Chikanga to their activities. The prophet himself only ever requested that certain people consult with him and be shaved. He did not encourage the bewitched to seek revenge.

Various churches in Malawi and Tanzania disapproved of Chikanga, although some formerly critical Christian administrators became less dogmatic after encountering the famous healer in person. On the occasions when the large Presbyterian ministry from nearby Livingstonia appeared unannounced to conduct services among the hordes of people milling around Chikanga's village, the healer allowed them to preach, watching dispassionately. While he was clearly a threat to them, they did not disconcert him.

The churches tried hard to persuade their followers that Christian unction was preferable to being shaved by Chikanga. But a story which spread rapidly throughout the region that a Finnish Lutheran had been seen travelling by bus from Chikanga's village with fresh scarifications on his forehead, convinced Chikanga's followers that if white missionaries secretly believed in him, his spiritual power must be truly universal.

Chikanga's downfall – mainly the result of the anxiety his popular presence stirred in politicians – was blamed on a report from the Presbyterians which accused him of undermining the authority of the chiefs, stirring up feelings of fear and hatred through his emphasis on witchcraft, and threatening public health due to inadequate sanitation for the vast numbers of people who were constantly in his village.

Militant members of the Malawi Congress Party, resenting

the fact that Chikanga had not joined their ranks, tried on several occasions to disrupt his community. Chikanga insisted he had no interest in politics and wished only to use his powers of divination to help people. Eventually, he was summoned to Blantyre for an audience with President Hastings Banda, who ordered him to live near the capital where his activities could be monitored by state officials. Banda's relations with Tanzania soured in the mean while and border controls were tightened, making it difficult for much of Chikanga's following to travel to Malawi to consult him.

Regardless of political interference, Chikanga's influence would inevitably have waned over time as people began to realise that the poverty and misfortune he was supposed to eradicate along with witchcraft had not in fact declined. By 1965 rumours began to spread that Chikanga was cheating people and could no longer shed light on their miseries. It was clear that the career of a great African prophet was over.

* * *

The many messianic religious movements arising in Africa seldom attract attention outside their own ministries unless they become doomsday cults or significant political parties. An interesting one in Congo, with radical motives and plagiaristic methods, began as a religious phenomenon but quickly assumed a political agenda, becoming the basis of a rudimentary nationalism.

Like other forms of messianism, it displayed features of a moral and spiritual revival. But it was also a reaction against colonialism in general, and the manner in which Christianity had been imposed on Africans in the region in particular.

Christianity in Congo around 1920 was characterised by intense rivalry between the Catholics, who saw themselves as the national religion because of their close connections with the government of the day; the Protestants, represented by Swedish evangelical missions and viewed by the Catholics as foreigners; and the Salvation Army. The Congolese found themselves torn between Christianity and their own traditional religion, on the one hand, and offshoots of various Christian churches who were openly at war, on the other.

Into this hiatus stepped the imposing figure of Simon Kimbangu, who soon became known among his followers as 'the Saviour'. Born in 1889 at Nkamba in the Belgian Congo, he had been educated at a local Baptist mission station where he acquired a particularly good knowledge of the Old Testament. After failing to pass the examinations to qualify as a pastor, Kimbangu was suddenly 'touched by the grace of God' in March 1921, and was thereafter recognised as a gifted healer.

Rapidly achieving a reputation as a miracle worker, he began to model himself on Jesus Christ, his village becoming known as the New Jerusalem. Kimbangu referred to himself as Prophet, Messenger of God, and Son of God – obvious symbols of the Holy Trinity – and he began calling himself Gounza, which means 'all these at once'. A talented teacher, he gave lectures about his new movement, first in the neighbourhood and then further afield. Before long, his devoted disciples included both Catholic and Protestant catechists as well as African pastors, who were proud to have a messiah belonging not only to their own ethnic group but also to their traditional religion (albeit now liberally infused with Christianity).

In addition to being created in imitation of Christ by a prophetic personality whose message referred to a golden age, Kimbangism was a typical witch cleansing cult. Simon Kimbangu campaigned far more successfully than the missionaries before him for the widespread destruction of magic figurines and totems. His claim that witchcraft was the cause of society's ills was readily accepted and its denunciation welcomed by his followers. In some areas, his disciples went so far as to publicly identify witches as those people whose hair did not absorb the water when baptised.

Kimbangu's ritual included sermons – often highly politicised – with accompanying hymns, confession and baptism. At no stage did he try to interfere with ancestor worship, which retained a central role in his services. His following grew so rapidly that the Belgian administration, alarmed by his popularity as well as incidents of 'aggressive xenophobia', decided to intervene.

Simon Kimbangu was arrested in September 1921. Initially condemned to death, thereby achieving instant political martyrdom, he was later pardoned and deported to Katanga.

The mythology surrounding Kimbangu grew. He was not only Gounza, an extravagant expression of his personal divinity, and the Saviour, which asserted him as the political liberator of the Congolese, but also Simon the Great because of the apocalyptic catastrophes he might unleash in the process of creating 'the Kingdom of God'. Later, he became 'King and Saviour of the Black People', by which time he himself was no longer portrayed as Christ-like but as the founder-martyr of a truly indigenous religion, free of foreign control. 'God promised us to pour out his Holy Spirit upon our country. We besought him and he sent us a Saviour of the Black peoples, Simon Kimbangu. He is the leader and Saviour of the Black people in the same way as the saviours of other races, Moses, Jesus Christ, Mohamet and Buddha.'

Kimbangism's inspiration veered between Jewish theology and Christianity, while drawing heavily on Salvation Army organisation for its hierarchical structures. The notion of a supreme being, not central to traditional African religion, came and went.

Separated from his following, Kimbangu contributed little to his towering image. It was the organised repression of the Belgian authorities that propelled his movement to greater and greater heights. Having given Kimbangism a political martyr, the government proceeded to endorse the idealisation of its leader through the denunciation of Simon Kimbangu, while the leader himself remained forever heroic, under no obligation to be judged in the flesh.

By 1939, Kimbangism had acquired a new leader called Simon-Pierre Mpadi, although Kimbangu remained its idol-in-exile. Mpadi gave the movement a new name, *Nzambi ya Khaki*, meaning Khaki God – a reference to the colour of the disciples' dress, which Mpadi called 'the uniform of hope and victory'.

The new church broke still further away from the European missions and from traditional African religion, except in its acceptance of ancestor worship. An official sermon began:

> The pictures you are shown, and which you take to be photographs, are inventions of the white man. Neither in the time of Jesus Christ nor of Adam was there any such thing as photography. The crosses that you see all over the Congo are contrivances of Satan, for the true cross was in Judea and Jesus was taken down from it: never kneel before a cross. The Jews who belong to the church of Moses have no pictures of crosses in their churches, and we don't want any either. Moreover, God has separated us from Jesus Christ and given us a Black Saviour, whom the whites shot dead, or tried to . . .

The objective of the new approach was to regroup and unite the maximum number of Congolese, and it succeeded.

Khakism grew and grew.

Out of its confused doctrine came a commitment to a sort of religious federation while at the same time, because of its opposition to colonialism, to a kind of religious racism. Despite the stated move away from established 'foreign' religions, Khakism continued to imitate.

While its philosophy may have been muddled, Khakism's popularity was clear. Church attendance swelled, with services becoming occasions for psychological liberation rather than simple spiritual reflection. The hymns took on a new, lively rhythm, sometimes accompanied by drums, clapping and even dancing. The sacred traditional African ceremony, during which troubled people became possessed and went into noisy, unruly trances, was a common feature of the liturgy.

No organisation founded on Congolese initiative had ever been so successful. It spread hope of an imminent end to the alienation experienced under colonial and missionary influence, offering a new beginning free from poverty and insecurity. Modelled as it was on the universality of the Christian church, Khakism created a form of social reorganisation that extended the limits of ancient African clan structure. This pointed the way to the creation of an even larger political group, extending beyond tribal and national boundaries. Once the colonial authorities understood these potentially subversive characteristics, they feared a nationalist upsurge and moved swiftly to silence Khakism.

Further north in Africa during the same period, Nuer, Dinka and Lugbara prophets also drew from traditional African beliefs to form prophetically inspired political resistance movements. Apart from introducing new levels of organisation and new symbols of unity, these quasi-religious movements formed the basis of much of the nationalism of

Africa's pre-independence era.

However, the popularity of prophets like Kimbangu owed less to burgeoning politicisation than to the mythical expression their movements gave to the hopes and fears of ordinary Africans.

Three

On the Trials of Being a Witch

The witch's life is not a happy one. From the moment of accusation, she embarks on a nightmarish journey into a world of malice and mayhem where popular belief becomes her reality.

Accused again and again of evil deeds she did not commit – on the basis of circumstantial evidence and random accusations – the witch often embraces her role as a denizen of destruction and behaves accordingly. Some psychiatrists believe schizophrenia arises from a similar sequence, based on society's imposition of a multitude of roles upon an individual.

Zimbabwean anthropologist M F C Bourdillon, in *Where Are The Ancestors?*, explains:

> Witchcraft beliefs provide a rationalization of suspicion and tension. Although to the modern western mind these beliefs may appear as irrational superstitions which can divide a community or bring unjust approbrium on persons who have fallen victim to vague suspicion, to the Shona mind the beliefs are based on a real experience of the world about them. Evil, troubles, sickness are undeniable and demand explanation; social tension and conflict frequently arise, a clear sign that some people are careless of the good of their neighbours; bad people are to be found and appear at times to have their way.

Another anthropologist, J R Crawford, points out that once an accusation of witchcraft has been made, 'a chain of events may be set in motion which can lead rapidly to the most unforeseen and often tragic consequences'. The accusation is the means by which an entire community participates in what usually began as a private quarrel; it then becomes a device for marshalling public opinion against an individual. Aptly described by Crawford as a 'strategy of attack', witchcraft accusation prevents members of the community from remaining neutral towards the conflict because everyone accepts that witches, being intolerably anti-social, must be exposed and punished.

Witchcraft beliefs are infinitely rich in symbolism. The 1965 Zimbabwe murder trial testimonies in this chapter contain many clues to the complex ideas of evil embodied in the Karanga culture of the two women describing their bewitching deeds to the court. For example, the birth of twins or a handicapped child are inevitable portents of witchcraft in Karanga society. God creates only normal infants, the Karanga believe, so such a birth indicates evil influences. In the case of twins, God gives only one soul because there is only one God. The birth of two babies cannot therefore be God's creation.

The fantastic world of the witch, who is often a person

suffering from mental illness, is a cruel and treacherous one. As a result of the following testimony in the murder trial of Ndawu, a self-confessed witch, a Zimbabwe court found her guilty, with extenuating circumstances, of killing a small child named Shani, who died from a fractured skull. The corpse had a circular piece of skin missing on the left cheek, and some skin had been removed from the vagina. Ndawu was sentenced to two years in prison.

The dead baby's mother, Muhlavo, gave evidence to the court about the witchcraft activities she had engaged in with Ndawu, to whom she was related by marriage:

'Before my menstrual period began I visited a certain woman whose name was Tsatswani in order that she might instruct me in midwifery and sex matters in general. This lasted for about a month. At the end of the course some beer was brewed to mark the end of the course. On that day Tsatswani took me down to the river and there cooked some porridge and put into it little things that looked like small black stones. It was all to do with witchcraft.

I slept at Tsatswani's room and later that night I saw a light in the doorway. There was a fire outside the door and I went outside; there I saw two things but I do not know what they were. On the following day I was sick. Tsatswani said that was a sign that we should indulge in witchcraft together. This was all at the end of this week. I then went home to my kraal.

I was at this time a member of the Zionist Church. I was also sick. I went to the church and asked about this sickness. I testified as to what I had seen on that night at the end of the course with Tsatswani. I was told that I was a witch. I believed this.

Some months after this I married Chidava. My first-born

was Machanja. At about six months he became ill and died. I went with my husband to find out the cause of his death to Tsilmele, a healer. Tsilmele said that my child had been bewitched by people in the countryside.

I know an African woman by name of Chirunga. She is a witch. We have been out at night bewitching people. We have gone out five times. The accused, Ndawu, came to my hut one day and said she wanted to be friendly with me. Later she came again and we went to the fields and there I made certain incisions on the accused's hips. I applied some magic to these cuts; some white medicine. This was the same stuff that Tsilmele had given to me some years earlier. The accused was at this time quite a young girl, not yet married and still living with her parents.

I explained to Ndawu that this meant she was now a witch. I explained that we should go about at night bewitching people.

Once I went out with Chirunga and the accused to see my husband. They both came to my hut . . . They came riding on hyenas at night. We all went to my husband's hut. They came to me in order to bewitch my husband Chidava. This was also to teach the accused (how to be a witch). I cannot explain the reason for this. It came to us as a dream.

We poured some sweet beer into Chidava's mouth. There was some bewitching medicine in it. We then sprinkled some more medicine on his body. We then left and I went to bed. The accused and Chirunga then took their hyenas and rode away into the night. Three days later my husband died.

A little later my two friends, the accused Ndawu and Chirunga, came at night on hyenas, and we all went to the place where the body was buried. We exhumed the body of my husband. We skinned the body. We cut a piece of the meat and took it to my hut. We replaced the body in the grave. At the hut we took the meat and ate it. It was good.

Some time later we three went to visit Meke, the brother of Chidava. We all rode hyenas. Near the kraal we talked amongst ourselves and decided to kill Meke. We went into the village and found him sleeping. Each of us laid hands on him. The next morning Meke was ill. The kraal head then came to us and said that we should not bewitch Meke. So we relented and Meke lived. After this the accused married and went to live elsewhere.

Quite recently myself and the mother of the accused, Keysai, were attending a beer drink. A report was made to us (about Keysai's daughter) and we left and went off to find the accused.

Two days later I went to visit the accused in Chief Maranda's area. I went at night on a hyena's back. I stood outside the hut where the accused was sleeping. I went inside and then we both came out together. The infant was in the accused's arms. I got hold of the legs of the infant and the accused its arms. We pulled the body, and later I rode off on the hyena. I wanted to bewitch the child. I cannot tell the reason because it only came to us if we were dreaming. We fought over the child. We wanted to bewitch the child so that it would die. We wanted to eat it. The child was never dropped during the struggle. I then returned to my kraal.

At this time I was living in the lands in a shelter, protecting the crops. I lived in (this) shelter alone with my three children, Wani, Shani and Musiwo. Shani is the deceased in this case.

I remained in this shelter for three days after seeing the accused. At night on the fourth day after seeing the accused, her mother Keysai came to see me, brought the child, put it down in front of the doorway and left without saying anything. Ndawu remained. I asked why she had come. She indicated the child was sick and was not sucking. It was her intention to stay at the shelter. I reported to my brother Danana that there was a person with a sick child at the hut. He came to the hut and later left.

On the next day I went to the kraal head . . . The purpose of the meeting was to decide about Ndawu bringing the child to my hut. The meeting decided that I should stay with the accused.

On the night of the following day the infant died. At the time the infant died the accused was sitting at the door of the shelter nursing the child. The child actually died in my presence. I sent the accused with Wani to report to the headman. They returned to the hut but the headman did not come.

We spent the whole day with the dead child and on the next day I went to report to Chief Neshuro. I went before sunrise. I went with Musiwo, leaving Ndawu, Wani and Shani in the shelter. They were all sleeping outside the hut when I left. My two children were together but Ndawu was apart from them. There was a fire between them. Ndawu was awake when I left but the two children were asleep. I told Ndawu where I was going.

I went to Chief Neshuro and made a report to him. I returned to the hut in the lands. On arrival I found that my child was dead. Shani was dead. Danana was present, also Meke, and in a little while the accused arrived with her mother. Wani was in the garden crying. The policeman for the Chief was also present.

The accused could have bewitched my child instead of killing her with a stick, like a beast.’

Wealthy South African traditional healer Conrad Tsiane sees up to 70 troubled people a day. By throwing magic divination 'bones' and studying how they fall, he gleans mystical insights into his clients' problems.

Overleaf: Some traditional healers exorcise evil from possessed individuals by absorbing the demon spirit into their own bodies. Here, famed Namibian diviner Katjambia conducts an exorcism ritual in which she dances and prays for six hours.
(©Angela Fisher/Carol Beckwith)

Cattle – the source of wealth, marriage dowries as well as food – are the inspiration of life in many African societies. The Dinka man in Sudan lovingly protects his long-horned cattle from predators and raiders. (©Fabby Nielsen)

Previous spread: White chalk paste decorates the bodies of young Masai warriors as they approach the climax of the Eunoto ceremony. It takes place once every seven years in a location chosen by a diviner, to which the young men travel great distances in order to honour their heritage in the Great Rift Valley, Kenya. (©Carol Beckwith/Angela Fisher)

Gelede mask ceremonies performed by the Yoruba people of Nigeria are comic spectacles designed to illuminate social and spiritual control. The person masked dances to the rhythm of drums: despite the beat and body motion growing increasingly frenetic, the head remains utterly still, a model of calm contemplation. This conveys the Yoruba ideal of patience and peace in a turbulent world. (©Angela Fisher/Carol Beckwith)

The Bedik of Senegal hold an annual Minymor festival in which the spirit world appeases the powers of nature, blesses crops and expels evil forces. Masked figures like this one, covered with bark and leaves, communicate with the spirit world and are believed to maintain balance in Bedik life. (©Angela Fisher/Carol Beckwith)

The above testimony is of interest not only because it gives an unusual insider account – albeit a confused one – of witches' activities, but also because it highlights the challenges witchcraft poses for modern lawmakers.

Extensive cross-examination in this case of the witness, Muhlavo, failed to establish which parts of her evidence were factual and which were imagined as a 'dreamed' symptom of her bewitchment. The precise nature of the relationship between Muhlavo and Ndawu remained unclear at the end of the trial, so that it is not possible to establish from the evidence which social definitions were being clarified by the acts of witchcraft described by Muhlavo. Indeed, it is extraordinary that the court was able to pronounce any judgment at all from the muddled picture of events and non-events presented to it.

However, this evidence helps the reader to appreciate how difficult a subject witchcraft is for the legal profession to comprehend and regulate. Among many problems facing courts required to believe the unbelievable is that the activities of witches, being invisible, are not empirically provable.

Few countries in Africa have legislatively challenged the assumption of colonial lawmakers that witchcraft does not exist and the way to deal with witchcraft belief is, therefore, to suppress it.

Further evidence from this trial is instructive because the accused related the story of her life as a witch to a doctor involved in the case – an unusual testimony in the annals of African witch confessions. Ndawu told the investigating medical officer, Professor Michael Gelfand of the University of Zimbabwe:

'I inherited the power of the witch from my great-grandmother, who was also a witch. I cannot help it. When her spirit possesses me, I make people ill.

My father died long ago, and I do not remember him. My mother and I were not close to each other. After menstruating for the first time, I began to walk in the night while I was sleeping and some people began to whisper that I was a witch. Then, with my eyes closed, fast asleep, I walked through a closed door. Then everyone knew I was a witch.

Since that time I have been confirmed as a witch by many healers who specialise in sniffing out witches. It was one of them who told me that the spirit of my great-grandmother on my father's side gave me the skill of witchcraft. When the spirit possesses me I go out naked at night on my hyena and harm people without knowing about it. When I wake up I sit at the door of my hut crying and cannot remember.

I did not have a lover before my marriage because all the boys knew I was a witch. I thought I had to stay by myself and go out only with other witches. I did not want to be a witch. Then I married my husband, who is a very short somebody, like a dwarf. He was already married with children. Others thought I had bewitched him. When his first wife moved away they said it was because I was a witch. Then she died and they said it was because I had bewitched her.

I had several children but one birth was twins and one of them died and one was abnormal, with a hump-back like a camel. My husband died and I moved from village to village. I could not stay in one place because there was always somebody saying I was a witch. My children and I were always running. They could not attend school and were miserable.

Sometimes the people in the village would ask me to come and heal a sick person and I could make that one better, but soon after there would follow an accusation of bad magic. Then there was this very bad case with the child. But before that another child also. I do not know why it is always with young children but I want to change it now. When this case is over I am going to sell my cattle and visit a very powerful healer to drive the spirit away.

That previous time with the small child happened after my younger brother asked me to ask his employer, who I knew, to give him more money for minding her cows. She refused. Her infant became ill. It seemed to get better after she took it to the hospital. The fever left but her brain was affected. She had fits, frothing at the mouth and crying all day and all night for no reason.

The child's family accused me. The village elders decided we should visit a famous witch-finder in Mozambique. The journey was long, five days, and the diviner immediately knew that I was the one. On the journey back they made me carry a large rock as punishment and they beat me with a stick the whole way. I fainted. They gave me water and made me carry on. They tried to make me ride on the back of a dog. Then they filled my blanket with sand and made me carry it. But I could not because it was too heavy and I fainted again.

Then they took me to the infant in hospital. It was having many fits. The nurses told me that the child had suffered from meningitis and came too late to the hospital so the brain suffered from the fever. They told this to the family also but they believed I alone was the cause. I do not remember doing it, but I believe I was the cause. They told me to exorcise the evil spirit from the infant.

I tried for six days to heal the child with prayers and medicines. Then the other mothers with children in the hospital heard I was there with this damaged child and a protest broke out during the night. One of them had seen a snake, a certain kind of snake that is a sign of witchcraft. The mothers were screaming. The children were screaming. The doctor told us in the morning that I should leave the hospital . . .'

***

It is difficult to describe witches without relating a rare account of a witches' trial by ordeal in second generation reportage. British journalist Mike Donkin, understanding this problem, was kind enough to allow the author to reprint in full an event which he was privileged to witness in Ghana in March 2000, and which he described in a London newspaper, *The Independent*:

'She kneels in the dust beside the spiky bush and circle of rocks which are the fetish shrine. Nestled in the lap of her faded wraparound skirt is the white chicken whose death will help decide whether Bapyama is a witch.

The priest, barefoot and wiry-bodied, pours a measure of local brandy onto the earth as an offering and makes his incantation to the gods. In the glow of the early morning sun it is their voice which this ceremony will make heard. The gods will prove Bapyama innocent or guilty.

Gathered and watching silently around the mud huts with their roofs of straw are more than 200 other middle-aged and elderly women who have already been tried and condemned. This is the community to which they have been banished for life – the witches village of Tendang, one of several scattered around remote northern Ghana.

The chicken squawks as Bapyama shuts her eyes and makes her prediction. She has to say how it will lie – on its face or on its side – when it settles for the last time. If her prediction is right the faith decrees that she has a witch's powers and must stay there.

"The fowl will lie on its side," she says, and must be fervently hoping she is wrong.

The priest sharpens his knife on the rocks of the shrine, takes the chicken from her and cuts its throat. With a last chant he tosses it onto the ground.

The chicken raises little dustclouds as it flutters its wings wildly. Every eye follows its desperate and then more feeble movements. It settles flat on its breast, with its neck and beak outstretched. Then there is one last flap and it lies dead on its side.

Bapyama has predicted correctly. The gods have spoken and there is no denying their verdict: she has the power of witchcraft. There is, however, one further test that amounts to a plea in mitigation. Bapyama looks less than eager but nods her assent.

Drops of chicken blood and a pinch of earth from the shrine are stirred with water in the shell of a gourd. The priest explains that this is a sacred concoction and the verdict it will cast is final indeed.

"If she drinks this and she is truly a witch she will die in a few minutes. If she does not die that shows she may not be a witch but is only possessed by evil spirits."

Bapyama raises the shell in both hands and drains the brew. She seems none the worse for it. Then she recounts why the people of her own village sent her to Tendang to face these trials.

"There was sickness, bad sickness and nobody knew why. Some neighbours pointed to me and said I was causing this because I was a witch. The chief of the village sent me here. I am very sad because I have had to leave my family. I do not think I will ever see them again. I believe my neighbours accused me because they were jealous. I had a good farm and we were doing well, selling our crops. Now I have nothing."

So what is Bapyama's view of what the tests revealed. Does she now believe she is a witch?

"Well, I said which way the fowl would lie and it did that. So I must have a witch's powers. But I drank the concoction and here I am, I did not die. Perhaps the priest can take the evil spirits out of me."

Whatever happens, Bapyama knows that like all the women in Tendang she will never be able to return to her home. Suspicions of witchcraft, once raised, are never forgotten. Theirs is a life sentence.

The first attempt to change the outlook for the women of Ghana's witch villages has come from the aid agency International Needs. After an initial fact-finding visit, its Ghana Director, The Reverend Walter Pimpong, plans a detailed study. There is a basic human rights issue to be addressed in a place like Tendang, he says.

"These women have lost everything they could count on. Their husbands and relatives have abandoned them. Their children have mostly been taken away. They have been banished to a desolate place with no way to support themselves."

Walking with him among the round huts, hand-made from sun-baked clay, confirms the hardship. One woman in her seventies stirs a handful of maize into a pot over a fire of twigs. Her single room is bare of anything but a few rags to wear.

A few women have brought their children and so have them

to feed and clothe as well. The children join the weary procession two miles to the river daily to fetch and carry water.

"The saddest thing is that once they are accused they are stuck here until they die," Walter Pimpong says. "They fear that if they went back to their own communities they would be killed and they are probably right. The beliefs . . . are deeply rooted."

The village of Nani is not far from Tendang but it feels a world away. As you walk in there are sounds of carefree family life, and there is laughter. Yet in the past decade or so the Chief of Nani has banished 14 women as witches.

Chief Zachari Mahama sits cross-legged on a leather cushion, with his male elders gathered beside him. In his purple robes he radiates power and confidence. When it comes to dealing with accusations of witchcraft, though, it seems his hands are tied.

"When my people declare that a woman is a witch I have to send her away for her own protection," the Chief says. "Otherwise she may be beaten to death. I am not happy to banish women but I am compelled to do so to keep the peace in my village. The tests are all done according to our faith so it would also be very hard for me to rule against the priests and defend someone they found to be a witch."

The Chief is pressed harder. Does he really believe that the 14 women he has banished were all witches? He adjusts the hem of his robe for a moment or two. "Yes," he says. "I am sure they were witches and they are witches now."

The government of Ghana is just as reluctant to act against these modern-day witch finders, human rights campaigners complain. Most Ghanaians may now count themselves Christians or Muslims but even among them fetish traditions may still hold sway. And all of them have votes.

"Only education will allow these women back into society," Walter Pimpong says. "If cholera kills people in a village they must understand that the problem comes from a disease that can be treated. If crops fail they must look for the reason in the soil. I am afraid, though, that this will take a long time and many more women will be condemned before then."

Back in the witches' village there is for one afternoon the surprising sound of music. Gathered in the shade of a tree, some women beat drums as others wheel, shriek and stamp in the dust. It is a celebration of the only sort ever held here – a funeral.

The body is covered only in a cloth and carried shoulder high from hut to graveside, where the fetish priest carries out his duties for the day. There is no family to mourn as the heat fades from the sun, but one woman of Tendang at least has been freed from her accusers, and has found peace. ’

Four

Healing the Wounds of War

Child soldiers have become a tragic feature of the war-ravaged recent histories of African countries like Sierra Leone, Liberia, Angola, Congo, Rwanda and Mozambique. Effective strategies for the relief of post-traumatic stress among abused children are urgently needed on the continent, but western psychologists seldom achieve appropriate interventions partly because – like most foreign care-givers – they are apt to westernise the problem in order to adapt it to their own understanding and training.

An attempt in 1994 by western-trained psychologists to heal post-traumatic stress in some of Mozambique's former child soldiers revealed the limitations of conventional trauma counselling in Africa.

The leader of the initiative, Dr Boia Efraime Junior, says of the early aspirations of project *Reconstruindo a Esperanca* (Rebuilding Hope), conducted on Josina Machel Island:

> Largely Mozambican by birth and western by training as psychologists, we arrived there believing that we were the primary resources of healing available to the children, their families and the community-at-large. We also arrived with a certain degree of faith in the diagnostic instruments and perspectives on psycho-traumatology we had acquired in our training. Our long-term relationship with the people of Josina Machel has taught us otherwise.
>
> It has forced us to expand both our notion of what constitutes psychotherapeutic intervention, as well as . . . its psychic integration. We found that the people of Josina Machel had healing resources . . . whose legitimacy and currency pre-dated our arrival by several centuries.

The experiences of the psychologists working on Josina Machel Island revealed not only how much knowledge has been lost in Africa partly as a result of earlier western prejudice against traditional beliefs in general and divination in particular, but also the unique way in which otherwise inaccessible information can be obtained through divination.

Few aspects of African life are untouched by divination so the process is critical to any study of Africa's cultures and its peoples – particularly cross-cultural psychology.

Mozambique – until 1975 a Portuguese colony – gained its independence after a bloody ten-year struggle spearheaded by the nationalist forces of Frente de Libertação de Moçambique (FRELIMO). Once in government, the socialist FRELIMO was challenged by the counter-insurgency forces of its rival, Resistencia Nacional Moçambicana (RENAMO). The resultant guerrilla war was especially bitter and destructive because, unlike the earlier colonial conflict, it did not unite the country against a common foe. Instead, a brutal civil war was exacerbated by South Africa's apartheid strategies as well as global cold war politics aimed at destabilising the entire region.

Although FRELIMO and RENAMO signed a peace agreement in 1992, and participated in democratic elections two years later, the conflict had by then claimed almost one million lives, 45 per cent of them children under the age of fifteen. The United Nations Children's Fund (UNICEF) estimated that 250 000 Mozambican children were suffering from psychic and physical traumas.

The children of Josina Machel Island, in common with the rest of the country, endured numerous experiences which put them at risk for debilitating traumatic stress. Boia Efraime explains:

> In addition to the fears and tensions of being in a constant state of danger for themselves and loved ones, some lost their entire families. Still others were kidnapped and put to the service of FRELIMO or RENAMO military. The Island's children were used in a variety of capacities, including as spies, to carry ammunitions, as soldiers on combat missions, as slave workers for the food production of soldiers, and as sexual concubines.
>
> Children's descriptions of the hardship and terror they faced during the conflict are only matched by the psychic scars which have remained long after the end of the war. People not only returned to villages that had been decimated materially, the war had also strained, and in some cases severed, many of the social ties which had been the glue of community well-being. Few families returned intact: husbands, fathers, mothers, daughters and sons had been lost in the conflict. Moreover, in many cases these loved ones had been killed by other members of the community.
>
> Brothers returned to their families, only to discover they had been compelled to fight for opposing forces. Teachers faced students who, only a few months earlier, they had witnessed

> bludgeoning family members. Young women, repeatedly sexually assaulted in military bases, now had to face their families and the shame and uncertainty of whether they would ever be 'marriageable' and, indeed, whether they themselves could ever consider marriage desirable.
>
> The children who had been kidnapped returned home to their parents or families, but still wondered how their parents could have failed to protect them. In their initial refusal to discuss the war with us or their children, we . . . discovered that parents wondered and agonised over the same question.

The biggest question for the psychologists at the outset, however, was how to win the confidence of the community and persuade individuals to share their traumatic experiences. An important breakthrough came when the funders of their project, *Reconstruindo a Esperanca*, began building permanent housing on Josina Machel Island. One boy told the psychologists: 'Now I can come to see you and tell you what is on my mind, because now you are my neighbour and I know that you will not go away.'

Says Dr Boia Efraime:

> In our initial attempts to provide them with counselling and support, we found that our diagnostic tools and therapeutic approaches were only of limited value. Conventional psycho-traumatology tends to focus on the individual's experience. Even when we do address the nature of collective trauma, we tend to approach the latter as if it were merely what emerges from the sum total of individual responses to traumatic events.
>
> We learnt, however, that trauma had insinuated itself into the very fabric of community life, but we could only get to the core of this dynamic by understanding the community cosmology or 'world of meaning'. This cosmology underscored people's understanding of what it meant to be healthy and sick, and our first lesson was that illness is not universally (seen) as an individual phenomenon.

> In the case of Josina Machel, an individual's state of illness or health was deeply tied to his or her relations (with) the community. This, in turn, underscored the importance of understanding the local sense of personhood: that is, where the sense of 'I' ended and 'we' began in our clients, their families and their communities-at-large . . .

Dr Efraime and his colleagues discovered that most of the post-traumatic stress symptoms exhibited by the former child soldiers 'had to do with being out of harmony with the spiritual ties that on Josina Machel linked the living and the dead. For instance, children reported either being haunted by spirits in nightmares, or reported an inability to make contact with the spirits of their ancestors. For them, this was taken to be a sign of falling from grace with their ancestors and, by extension, their family and community.'

It became clear to the psychologists that success in helping the traumatised children of Josina Machel lay in merging their own resources with those of the *curandeiros* – the Island's traditional healers.

The bulk of the rituals performed by *curandeiros* are designed to promote social reintegration. The ritual known as *Ku Phaha* establishes communication between a living family medium and the lineage ancestor spirits. 'The ceremony is conducted in the presence of family who wish to benefit from it and of others who only want to witness the fact,' explains Dr Efraime. 'At this ceremony, they must always have a traditional brew and snuff. The member of the family that speaks to the spirits takes a sip of the brew and spits it on the ground under a tree that the family normally uses as an altar for their ancestors.' The family medium explains the reason for the ceremony – forgiveness for evil committed during war – to the ancestor spirits and guides the family through a process of confession.

'Other families go to the *curandeiro* for a ritual called *Ku Femba* in which the healer, acting as a medium, establishes contact with bad spirits,' says Dr Efraime. 'These spirits are normally responsible for the disturbances in the family.'

Jonas, a former child soldier tormented by nightmares, told his haunting story to a traditional healer in 1995, in the presence of Boia Efraime. 'An excerpt from the *Ku Femba* performed on Jonas by the *curandeiro* Macuacua reveals the potent cathartic effect of this ritual,' says Dr Efraime, who documented the event.

> *Macuacua*: I cannot help you because you know . . . those people that follow you in your dreams. What I'm going to do is try (to have them) speak directly to you.

Macuacua then changed into his *curandeiro* robes, placed sacred necklaces around his neck and, holding a wand made from a cow's tail, approached Jonas, 'sniffing' around the boy for dead souls.

'All of a sudden, Macuacua (seemed) paralysed,' reports Effraime. 'His helper came to him and, singing softly, got hold of him and gave him something to smell. She then took the cow's tail from his hand. His aspect was completely altered. He was a medium and through him a spirit spoke.'

Macuacua:	You know me. I am the one who does not let you sleep.
Jonas:	But what have I done?
Macuacua:	What? Don't you know what you've done?
Jonas:	Are you that man from Xinavane that we caught after Bobole?
Macuacua:	It looks like you remember.
Jonas:	But if it's you, you know what happened . . . had to happen. If I hadn't done it,

	the commander would have killed me.
Jonas' mother:	But, who is this one? What have you done?
Macuacua:	Tell her; tell her everything.

Jonas then described the cause of his nightmares. He had belonged to a group of guerrillas responsible for hijacking cars on the national road. Their mission was to sever communication between the interior of the country and the capital, Maputo. The guerrillas ambushed the vehicles and set fire to them, after killing the occupants and stealing their belongings.

During one of these attacks, a man jumped out of the bus they were searching and ran into the bush. The commander ordered Jonas to follow the fugitive. When he found the cowering man, Jonas told him to stand up. He was about to shoot, when he realised the captive was a person he knew: a neighbour of his aunt – who Jonas called 'uncle' – at the stall where she sold vegetables in Xinavane. Jonas hesitated.

Another soldier arrived on the scene. Jonas lowered his rifle and said they were not going to kill the captive but use him as a porter to carry the goods they had stolen from the bus.

The group proceeded on a three-day march with several loaded porters, who were told they would be shot if they slowed their pace. Among the prisoners was a woman with a twelve-year-old son and a baby on her back. When the weight of the baby began to slow her down, a soldier told her to leave the child behind. She refused. The soldier seized the baby from its mother and, holding the infant by the feet, smashed her head against a tree. Everyone stared in horror at the tiny, inert body on the ground. The mother and sibling sobbed uncontrollably.

One of the porters dropped his load and tried to attack the

soldier who had killed the baby. He was struck on the head with a rifle butt, and fell. The commander came to investigate. He told Jonas to kill the porter lying on the ground.

> *Jonas (speaking to Macuacua)*: I had to do it with the knife because a shot could be heard in the area. The slaughter would serve as an example to the other prisoners. It was only after I had the panga (knife) in my hand that I realised the man I was supposed to kill was the one from Xinavane, my aunt's neighbour and the man I had saved three days earlier.

Jonas hesitated, unable to strike. The commander approached, demanding an explanation. Without looking into the face of his 'uncle', Jonas struck at his throat. The blow failed to sever the head from the body. A spurt of blood sprayed into Jonas' face, blinding him for a moment. The commander seized the panga and struck again.

> *Jonas (speaking to Macuacua)*: Those eyes, the eyes . . . the man's head next to the baby's body haunt me in my dreams . . . If I hadn't done it, the commander would have killed me right there . . . I had already saved your life, uncle. I had saved you when I found you in the bushes. I didn't want to . . .
> *Macuacua*: But you killed me. I cannot take care of my family now. How do you want me to leave you in peace? Who is sorry for me? I'm not a wild animal to be killed the way I was in the middle of the road and without a decent burial.

Jonas breaks down, sobbing.

> *Jonas' mother*: What did you want him to do? He was just a child. He was also captured by the *matsangas* (rebels) in Incoluane. They forced him to do those ugly things.

Jonas' father:	What are we going to do?
Macuacua:	Go and see my family, take my clothes and (give) me a burial. And then I want this boy to go and stay with my family for a year and help them plough the fields.

Says Dr Boia Efraime: 'Jonas and the family obeyed these demands. The burial was done. A year later, Jonas participated for six months in imaginative psychotherapy sessions. Like many other clients, Jonas spoke of the imaginary person who helps him, referring to his paternal grandfather, after whom he is named.

Explaining some of the ways he and his colleagues adapted imaginative psychotherapy to local beliefs, Dr Efraime says:

> In Mozambique, most children are named after a powerful family ancestor. People believe the child will come to embody many of the characteristics of this ancestor, and that this spirit is a kind of guardian angel who will protect the child throughout life. We built on this spirit to help children imagine a safe and secure place where they could go, and a safe and secure guide to whom they could appeal for assistance and spiritual support.
>
> We also broadened the therapeutic space by participating in local traditions that had significant therapeutic value, not only for the youth but for the community. For instance, we participated in *Karingana ua Karingana* – the practice of the community gathering around a bonfire and listening to the elders telling stories about the community's history. These story-telling sessions became an opportunity for people to share their war-time experiences. They enabled us to gain a much clearer picture of what the children and adults of Josina Machel Island had endured.

Bit by bit, the psychologists assembled the case histories of their clients. Carlota, a seventeen-year-old girl, told them:

'The soldiers would come during the night and take us to their homes or to the bush, where we were forced to sleep with them. Those who refused were shot on the spot. One girl from the village – she was very young, maybe six or seven years old . . . A soldier wanted to sleep with her and, seeing that her vagina was small, he cut her with the bayonet. This happened right before my eyes. He raped her and then left her to bleed to death. It was like that: we had to do what they wanted.'

Jonas, aged nine, recounted: 'They placed my family in the middle of the village and said they would kill us because my father was a teacher. They handed me a bayonet and ordered me to kill my father. I did not want to and started to cry . . . My father asked me to kill him because (that way) at least I would survive . . . I cried and, with my eyes closed, I plunged the bayonet into my father's stomach. I turned around and ran. A soldier caught me.'

Dr Efraime explains the guerrilla strategy in Jonas' case:

> By having Jonas kill his father in front of his family and neighbours in his own village, the guerrillas were trying to destroy all ties that linked Jonas to his past, his family, friends . . . and his village. As a guerrilla, Jonas could not run away because to run away implies having a place to go to. Jonas served for five years in the guerrilla forces.

Says Jonas: 'I was a good soldier, and was afraid of nothing during combat. All I knew was that death would free me from my nightmares. Life was a nightmare.'

In other cases, Dr Efraime explains that children were sent to the front line of conflict by their own families:

> This was no easy matter for children to negotiate and what was at stake, should they refuse, was equally compelling. For instance,

> when Filimone was 13 years of age, he was forced by his father to serve as a militia.
>
> His brother, Cesar, had been kidnapped by the guerrillas. What Filimone held most dear was the love he felt for his father, his family and his teachers . . . He (told) us that, had he not done what was expected (of) him, he ran the risk of losing that love and his parents' protection.

There was another traumatic dimension to the conflict of loyalty that haunted Filimone. He told the psychologists: 'During combat I avoided firing because I was afraid that one of my rounds could kill my brother, who had been forced to fight as well, only on the guerrilla side . . . To this day, there are places here on the Island that I do not go to . . . Those are the places where people who were killed by RENAMO are buried.

Insights achieved by *Reconstruindo a Esperanca* into the traditional beliefs of their clients enabled the psychologists to alleviate post-traumatic stress in many cases. But such creative interventions are rare in Africa.

At the annual congress of the Psychological Society of South Africa in August, 2000, Deputy Education Minister Father S'Mangaliso Mkhatshwa urged the country's predominantly white psychologists to learn 'at least one black language . . . given that psychology is traditionally known as "the talking cure" '. He told delegates there was a need to develop local models of care which were culturally centred and recognised 'the lived realities of our people'.

Five

Visions of National Suicide

The Xhosa people of South Africa came perilously close to extinction in 1857 because they believed in African magic. Theirs is an incredible story of the powerful esoteric knowledge provided by ancestral spirits, who embody universal wisdom in Africa.

The Xhosa were the first Bantu tribe encountered by early settlers in their advance up the coast of the Cape Colony. Frontier wars were fought between the British and the Xhosa, a proud people who had never been defeated by any Bantu group, including the Zulus under the mighty warrior Shaka.

By 1856, half a century after the British claimed the Cape colony as a permanent possession, five wars had been fought. Each devastated the Xhosa, who bore their early defeats stoically but finally slumped into a state of economic and spiritual turmoil as they were forced to surrender more and more land to the colonists. The last of the wars, three years earlier, had resulted in the loss of cherished Xhosa possessions, including the sacred Amatola mountains. Soon afterwards, a fatal bovine disease called lung-sickness – which was blamed on witchcraft – swept through the region, causing the tragic, choking deaths of vast herds of precious cattle.

While struggling to come to terms with their vanquished status and impending poverty, a new challenge rose up unexpectedly and brought the Xhosa nation to its knees.

Vividly described by Noel Mostert in *Frontiers*, it began one day in May 1856, when the fifteen-year-old orphaned niece of a diviner named Mhalakaza was sent by him to chase birds away from his cornfields near the cliffs above the Gxara river. Her name was Nongqawuse and she was accompanied by a younger friend.

The girls were climbing down to the gorge to swim in the river, when they were startled by two strangers who appeared suddenly from nowhere and identified themselves with names of men long dead. They told the girls to advise everyone in their kraal that a great resurrection was about to occur. It would help the Xhosa to drive the white people away provided, as a sign of faith, they destroyed all their cattle and all their crops.

The girls were told that new cattle kraals must be built for herds that would appear miraculously from under the ground; houses must be constructed for new people who would arise from the dead; grain bins must be dug for abundant new crops. Once these preparations had been completed and every head of cattle slain, the new people would rise up and sweep the conquering whites into the sea.

The girls rushed home to tell their tale, but no one believed them. The next day they went again to the fields and again met the two ancestors, who were dismayed to hear their prophecy had been scorned. Nongqawuse was told to bring her uncle Mhalakaza to the gorge four days hence, once he had sacrificed a beast and ritually bathed himself.

Convinced that the description of one of the prophets fitted his deceased younger brother – Nongqawuse's father – Mhalakaza obeyed the instructions and hurried to the pool where the ancestors, now invisible, spoke through the medium of Nongqawuse. Mhalakaza was told to convey the prophecy to Paramount Chief Sarili and the other Xhosa chiefs: they must kill their cattle immediately to make way for new disease-free herds.

Mhalakaza was no ordinary Xhosa diviner. He had a few years earlier formed an unlikely friendship with an unusual European named Charles Merriman, the Archdeacon of Grahamstown, whose task it was to organise the Church of England in remote areas of the Eastern Cape. Merriman employed Mhalakaza as his servant and interpreter and set out to explore the territory with Wilhelm Goliat – the name adopted by Mhalakaza during the time he served Merriman.

Merriman, described by the writer Lord Robert Cecil as 'excessively eccentric and thoroughly free from conventionality', decided to journey on foot. He and Goliat walked forty miles a day, talking all the way because Goliat was fascinated by Christianity and asked endless questions in halting English. Goliat already knew the Creed, the Lord's Prayer and the Ten Commandments in Xhosa. While journeying with Merriman he learnt some of the Anglican liturgy and being 'very tolerably informed in Biblical knowledge, and . . . a good man', Merriman confirmed him into the Church of England, the first Xhosa to take the Anglican communion.

When they returned to Grahamstown, Goliat built himself a hut in Merriman's garden but the relationship between English archdeacon and illiterate Xhosa changed. It was no longer the intimate companionship they had shared while tramping through the bush discussing philosophy. Merriman's wife noted that Goliat was 'dreamy' with a great desire to be a 'gospel man': she said that he retreated into a world of his own once he was urbanised. In 1853, deciding he no longer wanted to be Merriman's domestic servant, Goliat returned to his family kraal on the Gxara river in Paramount Chief Sarili's region and reverted to the name Mhalakaza.

After hearing the prophecy of the resurrection in the Gxara gorge, Mhalakaza began killing one of his own cattle each day. Many of his people followed his example. Soon the slaughter spread to other communities as more and more people embraced the heady prospect of the diseased animals being replaced by new herds.

It was not the first time African prophets in the then British Kaffraria had called for such drastic action in the hope of converting despair into optimism. Belief that the sacrifice would deliver a miracle had been held by at least five seers before Nongqawuse, all of whom had urged the Xhosa to stop cultivating and to destroy their cattle so as to achieve renewal. On those earlier occasions there had been no popular response to the prophets but now an epidemic of lung-sickness, with much talk of preventive slaughter, had inspired confidence in assertive faith. Once reports spread of Nongqawuse's regular communication with the new people, popular belief in the resurrection was sealed, not least because lung-sickness had reached the herds of Paramount Chief Sarili in the Transkei. As leader of the entire Xhosa nation, Sarili declared his belief in the prophecy. Once his powerful endorsement was known, the tragedy became unstoppable.

Sarili represented the main line of hereditary descent within the royal house of Tshawe, to which all Xhosa chiefs belonged. Over six feet tall, elegant and approachable, he was distrusted by the British, whom he had no reason to trust either. His father Hintsa had been cruelly killed by the commando of a British governor, Sir Harry Smith, a man who felt so superior to Africans that he attempted to make Xhosa chiefs kiss his feet as a mark of respect. Sarili was a traditionalist who tried hard to curtail intrusive missionary and other white influence upon his people, the Gcaleka. He saw no reason to adopt the white man's ways, including the wearing of clothes. Sarili maintained that the body odour of Africans in clothing was foul because they didn't change their garments often enough. 'I can't stand the smell of the dressed native,' he declared.

Sarili was in no other respect openly hostile to the colonists, yet they saw him as the 'fomenter' of recent wars. Once his central role in support of the resurrection movement became clear, the British believed it to be a plot by Sarili to raise the Xhosa nation in a 'combination' against the colony.

From Sarili's point of view, it was not surprising that he supported the prospect of a miracle when shown its possibilities. The frontier Xhosa had been pushed so far back by the British that they saw no plausible military retaliation, and the insensitive British were adding insult to injury by striding authoritatively across the territory, undermining Xhosa chieftainship through Sir George Grey's newly appointed magistrates. Meanwhile, the Xhosa nation's wealth in cattle was being destroyed by lung-sickness.

There was another factor influencing Sarili: he had great faith in the Russians, thought to be the Xhosa's ancestors, who were believed to be the new people due to appear in the promised resurrection. This illusion developed because the Xhosa had heard about the Crimea and knew that the war in Europe had gone badly for the British. Sarili had questioned Archdeacon Merriman intently on the subject when the Englishman visited his Great Place, assuring him that the Russians were coming to conquer the British in South Africa. The news spread quickly among the Xhosa who, believing all of England's enemies were black, began to think of the Russians as black, too. Some desperate Xhosas took to sitting on coastal hills in the hope of spotting Russian ships arriving on the horizon.

Sirili's readiness to embrace the notion of resurrection as a solution to his nation's troubles probably owed much to his own tragedies. Most of his heirs had died, the last a much-loved twelve-year-old son in 1853.

Spurred by all these influences, the cattle killings spread steadily. The colonists watched in astonishment, unable to reconcile the Xhosa's intense love of their cattle with a delusion demanding the death of the valued herds.

One of the British administrators, Charles Brownlee – an unusual white man in Africa because he had learnt the local language – was sympathetic to the deeply religious Xhosa's predicament. He tried hard to dissuade Sirili and Chief Ngqika from their disastrous belief in African magic, telling his sceptical wife one night in 1856 of his foreboding. 'I fear (they will kill their cattle). Then there will either be war or you will see men, women and children dying like dogs about your door.'

Although Brownlee was the colonists' best hope of communication and influence with the Xhosa people, his superiors were paranoid about Sarili's motives and distrusted Brownlee's sympathy for the Africans. Lieutenant-Governor John Maclean began to assemble a complex network of paid informers, many of whom cynically endorsed the British belief that Sarili was trying to start another war. The Xhosa, meanwhile, began to split into two groups, Believers and Unbelievers.

When Sirili had earlier declared his faith in the prophecy, he had travelled to Gxara to verify the coming resurrection. Afterwards, Charles Brownlee spoke to those who claimed to have witnessed Sirili's encounter with the supernatural. The Paramount Chief was said to have been shown his beloved recently deceased son as well as a favourite horse, long dead. The witnesses were particularly impressed that Sarili had seen and spoken to the dead.

Brownlee wrote:

> It seems absurd that shrewd and reasoning people . . . should be led astray by such reports . . . and that they should be giving up a certainty for an uncertainty, but if we reflect on some of the wonderful delusions in our own land in the last, and present, century . . . some measure of astonishment may be removed that a superstitious people, who have always regarded their chief doctors as inspired, should be led astray when the delusion is pleasing and its realisation desirable.

More and more people made their way to Gxara to verify the prophecy. As their anticipation increased so, too, did the cattle killing, and Mhalakaza announced the period of the full moon in July 1856 as the time of the great event. Excitement rose to a crescendo, but nothing happened on the appointed day.

The high esteem in which the Xhosa held their cattle is exemplified in the saying *Inkomo luhlanga, zifile luyakufa uhlanga*, which means 'Cattle are the race, they being dead the race dies'. Sarili and his followers' deep grief at the animal sacrifice required of them was spiritually eclipsed only by their awe of the ancestors who had appeared at Gxara to Sarili and subsequent pilgrims.

Nevertheless, when the July moon failed to deliver the miracle, Sarili's belief faltered. He called a meeting of his councillors to decide whether they should continue killing herds and destroying crops. Messengers were dispatched by the Paramount Chief to Mhalakaza, demanding an explanation. Mhalakaza replied that the new people had gone into a stronghold to await completion of the sacrifice, and he made a second prediction for the coming of the new people and cattle: the next full moon, one month hence.

Sarili was satisfied. The pilgrimages to Gxara continued, as did the cattle killing. Some of those who went to the river gorge were shown faraway figures in the sea and told they were the new people floating patiently in the ocean, waiting to deliver the miracle. They were told to listen carefully in order to hear the new cattle herds bellowing underground. Most believed what they were told by Mhalakaza and Nongqawuse. A few came away full of scorn and were shunned by the Believers, who viewed the shrinking numbers of Unbelievers as enemies compromising their own sacrifices.

Early in August a mist rose unexpectedly in the Gqunukhwebe region and people rushed home, believing that the predicted Day of Darkness had come at last. Word spread that the prophets wanted the whole Xhosa nation to assemble, wearing white blankets and new brass bracelets, on the day of the full moon. Two suns would rise over the Amatolas and collide above it, creating the Day of Darkness. The British would walk into the sea, which would divide to reveal a road for them to march along, back to the place of creation where they would meet their fate.

The Believers claimed the new world would emerge after the Day of Darkness. A jubilant resurrection of the ancestors would be followed by herds of new cattle appearing from under the ground. Only the ancestors of Unbelievers would not arise. The resurrection would restore the sight of the blind; the lame would walk again. Old people would become young. Even household implements would spring miraculously from the ground. No one would have need to cry or struggle or work again.

By August 1856, the chiefs whose cattle were hardest hit by sickness had killed vast herds, whereas the Ngqika people hardly experienced the lung disease and their chief, Sandile, initially threatened to punish those who killed animals in the name of Nongqawuse. Brownlee took heart and began to explore ways of working with Sandile against Sarili. But when he discovered that some of Sandile's councillors had begun to believe the prophecy as the full moon approached, Brownlee grew pessimistic and inclined towards the prevailing British view of a conspiracy. 'The evil appears to be near a climax,' he wrote. 'I think before the end of this month, it will be evident whether the storm is to pass over, or whether (they) are determined for a rush into the colony, for this may yet be the nature of Mhalakaza's order.'

The colonists prepared for war. Maclean felt that a Xhosa uprising against whites might be supported by the powerful Basotho leader Moshoeshoe in the north, and possibly by the Mfengu and the Ngqika. With less than 4 000 troops and disinterest in London, the British Commissioner anxiously contemplated the prospect of 35 000 Xhosa warriors. Brownlee tried to remain practical. 'Though famine may induce people to commit riots and outrage, a starving people are not in a position to undertake aggressive warfare; for (they) say that famine always did more to conquer them than the forces brought against them, and wars have never been begun in seasons of scarcity.'

Brownlee began a heroic initiative to stop the Ngqika from joining the Believers. Sitting down with Sandile to discuss the matter, the Englishman implored the Xhosa chief to accept Christianity's idea of resurrection. Sandile replied that he did not believe Mhalakaza because God would not work in a secret pact with him. He had told his people not to kill their cattle and would not do so himself. Even if darkness descended as Mhalakaza predicted and his own cattle were destroyed because he had not believed, Sandile declared that he knew God would be merciful and would again feed him because the sin he had committed in disobeying Mhalakaza was a sin of ignorance.

Sandile and Brownlee agreed to go together to persuade Sarili to stop the slaughter but Sandile's councillors rejected the idea, saying it was an offence against Xhosa custom for a lesser chief like Sandile to attempt to influence the paramount.

Shortly afterwards, the killing subsided abruptly when the predicted suns failed to rise and collide over the Amatola mountains. Instead, only the full moon rose and sank uneventfully. Sarili again confronted Mhalakaza, and also sent a message to Brownlee requesting a meeting. Brownlee was thrilled, especially when Sandile agreed to accompany him. But the Englishman – believing he could at last reason with Sarili as the single person capable of silencing Mhalakaza – had first to secure permission from his superior, Maclean, to attend the meeting.

Maclean remained emphatic in his view that 'superstition was made a means to a political end and that end was combined war on the white races'. More interested in driving a wedge between Sarili and Moshoeshoe, who were reportedly exchanging regular messages, Maclean was irritated by the request and instructed Brownlee not to accept Sarili's invitation.

Excitement in the resurrection revived in September, when Sarili returned to the Gxara gorge to hear Mhalakaza blame the second failure of the miracle on the fact that some Xhosa had sold rather than killed their cattle, angering the new people. Simultaneously, a rumour spread throughout the territory that a large number of well-armed new people on horseback had appeared from a river mouth and travelled along the beaches of the Transkei coastline.

Several reports described Sirili's visit to Gxara. One of them claimed that Sarili was told by Mhalakaza to sit and look steadfastly down on the ground in order to see the shadows of the new people. Sirili did as he was told, the shadows came as predicted, and Sarili was convinced.

Chief Mhala was told by Mhalakaza that he would be made 'quite young again', to his great joy. One of the colonists, Major Gawler, who hated Mhala, expressed surprise at the sudden change in Mhala's attitude. 'His former dull and frequently sulky and uncivil demeanour towards me . . . is now very civil, high-spirited and witty'.

Mhala was eager to become a Believer but his two senior sons opposed him. He decided to send a delegation of advisers to Mhalakaza at Gxara, where Nongqawuse refused to speak to them. On the third day, with an unusual mist over the water, they watched Nongqawuse walk a long way from them and then saw some indistinct figures. Denied permission to meet the new people and examine them more closely, they were told to go home and destroy their cattle and corn. The delegation returned to Mhala's Great Place to announce that eight of its nine members were now Believers, although they agreed that they had seen nothing. Mhala sent a message to Sarili saying, 'I believe and I am killing', although he denied this when questioned by his sons.

Sir George Grey sent a stern message to Sarili, warning him that the slaughter would result in chaos and starvation. 'I shall consider you as the guilty party and will punish you as such,' he said. 'You are the man that I shall hold responsible for what takes place.'

Sarili's reply came early in November. 'There is a thing which speaks in my country, and orders me and my people to kill our cattle, eat our corn and throw away all our witchcraft wood, and not to plant, and to report it to all the chiefs in the country.'

By the end of December 1856, after yet another full moon had failed to bring the miracle, the tragedy could no longer be averted, even by the constantly doubting Sarili. Brownlee had given up hope. There had been good rains but only the Unbelievers had planted. Vultures circled overhead. Fathers and sons, wives and husbands turned on each other as their beliefs conflicted. People openly disobeyed their chiefs when told to cultivate by Unbelievers. Xhosaland was in turmoil; the suicide of an entire nation was imminent.

Early in 1857, Sarili travelled to Gxara to consult Mhalakaza. He was told that the new people had been forced to disperse throughout the territory because some Xhosa still refused to kill. If the rising new moon in January was blood red, Sarili should immediately return to Gxara to witness the resurrection. If it rose yellow, the miracle would be delayed another month. Sarili, who was longing to see his deceased youngest son, was said to be so disappointed by this news that he would have committed suicide on the journey back to his Great Place had his councillors not hidden his spears.

Mhala claimed to have received a message directly from the new people: 'We said that all your cattle were to be killed. You have not done so. We leave you in disgust.' Within days, a new prophet had appeared in Mhala's region. Again a young girl, she claimed to have been playing in a pool on the Mpongo river when a man sprang out of the water alongside the heads of six cattle whose bodies were submerged. She made predictions similar to Nongqawuse's, to renewed excitement. The new people would appear on a hillside, opposite which was a matching hill where the Xhosa should hold a feast, she declared.

Fires were lit on the appointed day, meat cooked, beer brewed and drunk. Chief Stokwe, a Believer, took his favourite daughter to the celebration. Some time after midnight, one of the chiefs yelled out, saying he had seen the new people. Everyone clamoured to look.

'Now do you believe it?' Stokwe asked his daughter triumphantly. 'Did you see?'

'See what?' she asked.

'Can you not see the things on the other side of that hill?'

'No, I can see nothing but thorn bushes!'

Chief Stokwe was so enraged he threatened to kill the girl, while others leapt on their horses and galloped across to the hill opposite, expecting to greet their deceased friends and relatives.

The blood red moon of January failed to appear, and the mood throughout the Transkei grew desperate. Xhosa workers in road gangs had been reported 'saucily disposed' a month earlier by British supervisors, but they were now compliant and eager to hold on to their jobs. Thin and weak, subsisting at bonfires provided by those who still had cattle to kill, more and more began to look for work in the towns. Most, still hoping the miraculous new people would arise with the coming full moon, acknowledged that they might be dead by March if the latest prophecy failed to come true.

The British watched in amazement as tragedy engulfed the

Xhosa nation. Realising most of 'the enemy' were too starved to fight a war, Sir George Grey marvelled at the fortuitous self-destruction which would simplify British control over the Cape Colony. 'Instead of nothing but dangers resulting from the Kaffirs having during the excitement killed their cattle and made away with their food, we can draw very great permanent advantages from the circumstances, which may be made a stepping stone for the future settlement of the country.'

Much of the disappointment of the Xhosa themselves found expression in the hatred Believers felt towards Unbelievers in a war of recrimination that destroyed families as well as ancient tribal alliances. Believers were forbidden even to talk to those they felt had betrayed their great opportunity for renewal. Amazingly, Sir George Grey's government gave scant support to Unbelievers, much to the distress of Charles Brownlee who angrily protested that British protection for the Unbelievers could have saved thousands of Xhosa lives, particularly among Sandile's Ngqika.

Brownlee continued his struggle to prevent Sandile joining the Believers, but the battle was lost when the chief's wives and his mother threatened to desert him. Sandile was bewildered by countless stories claiming that the new people had been spotted all over the Transkei: their tents were seen rising out of the Butterworth river, starving people woke to find delicious bowls of porridge mysteriously delivered to their doorsteps, armies were seen sailing in umbrellas, long-dead people appeared suddenly from nowhere to implore their relatives to obey the prophets. Finally, Sandile succumbed to the pressure.

Brownlee went in search of Sandile after becoming suspicious at the news that he had moved from his kraal. He found the chief sitting beside a fire, surrounded by Believers. Usually saluted by the Xhosa, Brownlee was barely acknowledged and he knew immediately what had happened. Some of Sandile's most respected councillors had just been dismissed along with the men and women who continued to refuse to endorse the prophecy. They were all quarrelling furiously, and some began to attack each other physically. Brownlee tried to intervene but one of Sandile's advisers rounded on him.

'Why do you trouble with us?' he demanded. 'You tell us that hunger will destroy us – we will see . . . Leave us alone and do not trouble any more with us.'

Brownlee was distraught. With no alternative but to concede defeat, he sat down, buried his face in his hands, and wept. When he recovered his dignity and straightened himself up, Brownlee addressed the chief he had tried so hard to help. 'I now leave you, Sandile, with those whose advice you have taken in preference to mine.'

At the end of January, Sandile received a message that Sarili had seen vast numbers of disease-free cattle, sheep and horses, all of which were to be received by the Xhosa as soon as the killing was complete. Within days, Sandile had killed seventy of the ninety cattle in the royal herd.

A meeting of 5 000 Believers was called by Sirili in Butterworth to hear the final word on the resurrection. Chiefs and their subjects from all over Xhosaland camped in the area for several days. On February 1, a messenger arrived from Mhalakaza with instructions for the two-week period preceding the full moon.

They were all to return home and slaughter their remaining cattle, including the milking cows that were keeping many infants alive and the favourite beasts of deceased former chiefs, which were meant by hallowed Xhosa custom to die a natural death. The hides were to be dried and preserved for making doors for their huts as protection from the great storms that would precede the rise of the new cattle, and from the spirits seeking to punish Unbelievers. There would be two Days of Darkness before the arrival of the new cattle. On the third day, the sun would rise in the west, the sea would dry up or recede, the sky would descend to head height. A great earthquake would then release the cattle waiting underground. Both the new cattle and the new people would be immortal. Sarili was spellbound, asking one of the white traders present at the meeting for a supply of candles to light his way during the Days of Darkness.

Starvation now stalked everyone in Xhosaland. But Believers continued to walk tall, tightening their belts to quell the pangs of hunger and drawing strength from their conviction that the ordeal would soon be over. The resurrection must finally come in February, they reasoned, because they would not survive until the full moon of March.

Brownlee's wife, Frances, described the events of February 16:

> At dawn on the great day a nation, many of whom had doubtless not slept, rose joyfully, decked themselves with paint, beads and rings, to welcome their long-lost friends.
>
> One of the saddest sights was that of an old woman wizened with age, and doubly wrinkled by starvation, decked out with brass rings jingling on her arms and legs . . . The sun rose and made the circuit of the heavens, closely watched by expectant hosts in vain. He set in silent majesty in the west, leaving the usual darkness over the earth, and the black darkness of a bitter disappointment in the hearts of thousands.

A missionary observed: 'There was no heaving of the earth, no processionary march of cattle or of men, but only an unwonted stillness since now, for the first time during unnumbered centuries, neither the lowing of cattle nor the bleating of sheep was anywhere heard.'

One of Sarili's grandsons, a boy at the time, told a writer in later years:

> I sat outside my hut and saw the sun rise; so did all the other people. We waited until midday, yet the sun continued its course. We still watched until the afternoon and yet it did not turn, and then the people began to despair for they saw that this thing was not true.

Some Xhosas never lost hope and continued peering into their empty grain bins each morning to see if they had been filled overnight. One old man was found dead with his head overhanging the edge of his corn pit. He had knelt down with his last breath, recounted Frances Brownlee, and lacked the strength to rise again.

The aching disillusionment of the Xhosa and their slow deaths went on for many months. Frances Brownlee, who twenty years later said the experience still made her feel ill, wrote at the time: 'Oh! The pity, the heart-breaking grief, the sad horror of it all . . . The first sound in the morning and the last at night was the pitiful, endless cry for food.'

Bones from rotting cattle carcasses were gnawed by starving people. Children wandered about, dazed, combing the fields in search of edible roots. Preserved hides were boiled and eaten, including battle shields and leather garments.

People reaching soup kitchens in the towns looked like crumpled skeletons. A young English missionary, who supplied eighteen pots of food daily from his own purse, said: 'I never saw such a horrible sight. They could hardly crawl along. I was never so tempted to cry in all my life as I watched the poor little children crawling.' When he saw Sarili's son among those begging for food, his heart hardened and he told the starving man to go and ask Mhalakaza for help.

Mhalakaza and his family had already died of starvation in the appalling tragedy that had decimated the Xhosa population from 105 000 to less than 38 000 by the end of 1857. The country was 'silent and ghastly', wrote one missionary. 'Not a cock was left to crow.'

Although it is believed throughout Africa that they maintain society's equilibrium, the ancestor spirits had in these shocking events misled the Xhosa, betraying their trust by inflicting a deeper disaster than the combined calamities of war and disease would have done.

Six

Tsiane the Diviner

The most successful African healers achieve such popularity that they often become rich. One diviner in South Africa is so busy and so wealthy that he flies around the country, dispensing remedies for bad luck and ill health, in his own aircraft.

Another traditional healer with a thriving practice in South Africa is Conrad Tsiane, who sees up to seventy patients a day, seven days a week. At forty-two, he is young for his formidable reputation as both a diviner and herbalist – known locally as a *sangoma* – to thousands of people, some of whom travel for days to consult him. He admits to being wealthier than he ever dreamt possible in the days when he qualified as a schoolteacher.

His double-storey house rises like a palace amid the humble

dwellings at Moutse, a two-hour drive from Pretoria. It contains plush suites for the 'important ones who might want to consult in private', with crystal chandeliers gleaming overhead, bold floral carpet running riot up the walls to the ceiling, satin linen and luxurious bathrooms. There is a large framed photograph of Conrad Tsiane in traditional dress standing outside his house with Nelson Mandela, then president of South Africa, and another of the healer with Thabo Mbeki, the current head of state. Both of these illustrious visitors came to Moutse to greet Tsiane in his capacity as mayor of the region.

He smiles agreeably when asked if the presidents solicited his divination powers. 'Our people believe,' he says. 'Definitely, our people believe.'

Conrad Tsiane discusses the diverse divining processes through which inaccessible spiritual information is obtained in Africa, explaining that the diviner's body sometimes becomes the vehicle of communication during spirit possession. Some systems, especially in West Africa, require the diviner to interpret cryptic metaphoric messages. Most divining processes involve symbolic items being shaken in some form of diviner's basket. Tsiane uses all these methods of esoteric enquiry.

Some traditional healers are charlatans, he admits, explaining that in the past there were only a few healers treating thousands of people, whereas today they 'spring up in every village. The standard of training has declined and some are lying or guessing. But the people know when traditional doctors are liars trying to make money with no interest in healing. They don't punish the one who is a cheat these days, even if he refuses to give their money back, but they will boycott that sangoma. Then everybody knows the person cannot be trusted to tell the truth.'

Behind Tsiane's house is a paved courtyard lined with wooden benches where his patients wait for him in the sunshine. Many are too poor to afford bus fares and have travelled the dusty roads on foot. There are rows of small rooms which house forty trainee healers who live in a compound comprising consulting room, dispensary and an administrative office bordering the courtyard. Twenty-eight staff members assist Tsiane in his practice, including herbalists who chop up medicinal cures collected from trees, plants and animals. The trainee sangomas are there to learn and to be vigilant to their teacher's commands.

Conrad Tsiane is a charming man, articulate in many languages, relaxed and clever. He listens intently when you speak, his eyes staring hypnotically into yours. He tells the author he has informed the assembled patients that a researcher will be sitting in on the consultations, and none of them seem in the least perturbed by this breach of confidentiality. They are clearly enthralled by him.

Beside Tsiane in the consulting room is a large diary in which the patients' names have been listed by his secretaries. There is a brass bell to summon the patients and the trainees, who prepare prescriptions in the adjoining dispensary. A grass mat lies on the floor between healer and patient, on to which he 'throws the bones' in the divination process. Very few patients attend alone.

'In our custom, people believe in not telling you anything the first time they come to a particular traditional doctor. They come with others to see if you know the truth. If they're old clients they might tell you what's wrong and they might come alone. But if they're new they expect you to convince them and, if your diagnosis doesn't work, they can demand their money back.'

Tsiane rings the bell and the first patient of the day enters;

a middle-aged man, dishevelled, speaking in a quiet voice, eyes troubled. He tells his story briefly. Tsiane listens and translates. 'His wife has left him. He wants to know if they are still in love, her whereabouts and can he get her back?'

Lifting a hide bag containing his divining tools – a collection of small goat's bones, shells and stones – Tsiane gets up from his chair and walks to the patient, holding the bag open. The patient places his money inside and blows over it. Shaking the bag vigorously, Tsiane bends and spills its contents on to the mat. The patient leans forward, watching intently, as do several trainees crouched in the doorway.

Tsiane lifts a long perspex rod with which he points first to a shell and then to a collection of bones as he deciphers messages sent by the ancestors. Symbolically, he has shaken up society in his divining bag and is now re-creating and reordering that society.

'There were problems at home,' he tells the worried man. 'A sexual problem – she was not satisfied – so she fell in love with someone else. We can trace her because there was no witchcraft. We can help. We will tell her we can change him. We need some of her clothes to get in touch with her.

'He talks of bad luck,' Tsiane continues, 'but we've told him it's not witchcraft. He is unemployed. There is no income, which will result in a wife leaving. The only breadwinner is his mother, and her money couldn't cope with a large family. It is a simple problem. The missing wife must come here to see me. And he must get a job. We must cleanse him with medicine so he has normal sexual function.'

Tsiane rings the bell and four trainees rush in, falling to their knees in front of him. One grabs the bag and scoops up the bones, handing it back.

'If the trainees have questions about the consultations, they write them down and we talk in the evening,' Tsiane explains briskly. 'There is no time for interruptions now.'

He rattles off a prescription. Two novices jump up and run into the dispensary to prepare the medicine, laying a sheet of newspaper on the floor and taking scoops of ground herbs from rows and rows of plastic buckets standing on shelves stacked up to the ceiling. While they are wrapping the mixture, very quickly, Tsiane nods to the patient, who gets up and leaves.

There is no polite chit-chat in the style of old Africa here. Tsiane is neither concerned nor indifferent. He is simply businesslike; ringing the bell, collecting the money, dispensing the wisdom.

His next patient arrives, accompanied by a wife and an adult son. They sit together on the bench, watching the bones being thrown, hearing the diagnosis.

Tsiane explains: 'He has been here before. I sent him to the hospital to have his blood taken. He is a bit lame on the left side and I thought he had had a light stroke, which was confirmed in the report from the hospital. He has rough coughing and high blood pressure. According to the bones, he was not bewitched. I will prescribe more medicine, in addition to what he is taking from the hospital, for good luck.'

He rings for the trainees, who fall at his feet. While the medicine is being prepared, he tells the departing patient to return in three weeks.

'There is not much I can do for that patient,' he says, 'but our people want to come to traditional doctors, even if they also go to the hospital. They want to be in touch with their ancestors. This is a problem we have as traditional doctors.

If a patient comes with a broken leg, we know and they also know that they have to get that leg set in plaster at the hospital, but still they come to us first, for reassurance that there is no witchcraft. And for good luck from the ancestors. Many people believe that we don't refer our patients to clinics, but some of us do. They go if we tell them, but they come back to us.'

The next patient is an elderly man, accompanied by two sons. He tells Tsiane his family is troubled. They don't sleep well and suffer many minor illnesses. Tsiane throws the bones, which reveal that the patient's father died when he was a small boy in a distant part of the country during the 1920s.

'I've told him to go and find the grave so that we can exhume the remains and bring them closer to where the family is living. This is what the ancestors want. If he can't find the grave, he will have to come back and we will trace it. But he thinks he can find it. Sometimes we have this kind of problem and the grave has been buried under a construction or development of some kind. Then it is more difficult. We must perform some ceremonies for the ancestors.'

A father and son enter, the younger man looking startled. The father puts money in the bag and motions his son to blow over the bones. They scatter widely and Tsiane's voice is suddenly hoarse, crackling and fading to a whisper, as he points with his rod. 'The grandfather was a traditional healer,' Tsiane hisses, and the father nods. 'The son is possessed, unemployed, irritable since a car accident . . .' The father nods continually. 'He did not get hurt in the smash because it is the grandfather who has possessed him. He doesn't want to cause his grandson harm but he's warning him. The boy must ask forgiveness. We have to cleanse him, using the male goat as a sacrifice. If the ancestors don't take our goat, maybe this young man will become a traditional doctor.'

Tsiane taps himself on the chest. 'I experienced the same myself: complete confusion, everything upside down, couldn't concentrate, nightmares, and when I hated almost everybody because I was so angry and frustrated, I was told in my dreams where to get help. It was a traditional healer in Groblersdal who helped me, and the bad dreams were never again as bad. That is when I became a sangoma.'

Another two men enter and offer a fifty-rand note for Tsiane's services. When the diviner points out the fee is eighty rands, they look at each other in bewilderment. Tsiane waves the matter aside impatiently and proceeds, explaining to the author that the fee includes medicine, and sometimes 'orthodox remedies' that he buys in bottles from pharmacists in Johannesburg. One such is called *Umuthi Amandla*, a mixture to combat sexually transmitted illnesses.

'We see a lot of people with HIV/Aids, too many,' says Tsiane. 'Some sangomas offer medicine for curing this disease but others know it cannot be cured because there is no cure, even in the hospitals. I send everyone with this disease to the hospital for condoms and treatment because I can do nothing for these patients, and I tell them that. I tell them they must eat very well and protect their partners. I give them medicine for good luck but not to make them better.

'I think it is better for people to know the truth, and that is why you see so many people coming to me. I tell the truth. If more traditional healers worked with the doctors in the hospitals against HIV/Aids we would by now have succeeded in conquering it.'

Tsiane throws the bones for two diffident men now seated before him. 'They want to slaughter a cow to accompany a deceased relative to the ancestors,' he explains. 'They want to know that they are doing the correct thing for the ancestors. It's reassurance again: a very simple case.' He tells the two that everything is in order; the ancestors are satisfied. They look relieved as they leave, putting their hats on before stepping back into the hot courtyard.

Two boys tumble in next, giggling helplessly. Tsiane smiles and talks to them in a jaunty voice; a brief respite from the functional mood of the consultations. 'These have been sent by my uncle, also a traditional doctor,' says Tsiane. 'They have come to fetch medications for him.' He rings the bell and four novices hurry in, kneeling at his feet. 'You will notice that the trainees coming in today to mix the medicine are all men, although we have many women in training and in fact most sangomas are women. These messengers from my uncle are also boys, not girls. That is because some of the medicines can't be touched by menstruating women.'

Three women enter next, humbly bowed. A young, pretty one sits in the middle of the bench, flanked by her mother and mother-in-law. The older women explain the matter, addressing Tsiane earnestly. The young one looks defiant at first but then desperate and tearful when the diviner talks to her in short, urgent sentences. She responds quietly, her head down, tears spilling on to her clasped hands.

'This is a complex situation,' says Tsiane. 'This young lady has no husband: he has died. She must stay with her in-laws, according to our custom, safely in the hands of her mother-in-law. Both the mother and mother-in-law are in agreement here. The problem is the daughter. They want to check if she is bewitched, but the bones show there's nothing.

'The problem is she has a boyfriend, who she loves and wants to marry. But she cannot in our custom because her four children belong to the in-laws. They must stay with the mother-in-law and, because the children need their mother, she must stay also. I have told her that she is young and she needs to be loved and hugged and that is OK. She can have the boyfriend and do whatever she wants with him, except marriage. That is out because the mother-in-law does not want a husband living there who is not her son, and the young widow cannot go to live with a new husband somewhere else because she cannot take the children away from the mother-in-law.'

The telephone on Tsiane's desk rings and he speaks rapidly into it. 'Sometimes people want to consult by phone,' he explains as he replaces the receiver. 'My staff always put them through to me in case it is an emergency, a suicide call or something like that. But this caller dreamed that his ancestors sent him to me. His dream was a bad one. I told him he must come here and tell me, mouth to mouth. If there is something, I will feel it in my blood and see it in the bones. I cannot throw the bones when he is not here. He must come.'

Two women enter, the older one seating herself on the floor, legs stretched out beneath a blanket wrapped around several layers of garments. She has a defective eye, which gives her a crooked, suspicious look. She explains her plight carefully, gesticulating, while Tsiane listens to every word. When he proffers the bag, she struggles to remove money from its hiding place in the tight folds of a scarf bound around her head. The other woman leans forward to help. Tsiane waits, a dreamy look on his face.

'A very strange case,' he says eventually, while the patient is still struggling to retrieve her money. 'The son of this lady attempted to hang himself. I had tried to warn her; I saw someone was going to kill himself and I called to tell her. But she was not in that day. I talked to her sister and told her that this lady's son was trying to commit suicide. The sister didn't know what to do but somehow, through a force she could not explain, she decided to call the children much earlier than normally to gather wood in the morning, to kindle the fire for hot water before they went to school. They saw the young man trying to hang himself; the children, who had been woken earlier by the auntie, saw him trying to do it and they told the auntie and she stopped him.'

Tsiane throws the bones. The author asks the age of the woman's son. Tsiane says, 'Twenty-eight,' but then checks himself, counting shells lying on the mat. 'No, twenty-four,' he says and the woman nods. He discusses the bones with the patient and then translates.

'She has come to say thank you as her son would have been dead if I had not called the house. But she is still worried because the reason her son tried to harm himself is because he fought with his girlfriend and she did not want to be with him any more. Then, after he was saved from suicide, he went and tried to harm the girlfriend. I told her he needs counselling to show him he can still get another girlfriend and enjoy himself. That former girlfriend is not the only one.'

A family group crowds into the consulting room; two men bowing respectfully before Tsiane and two women, expensively dressed. They are the mother, father, husband and aunt of a young woman who died unexpectedly, cause unknown. The mother of the deceased removes a small purse concealed in her clothing when Tsiane proffers his bag of bones. As she drops the money and breathes over it, Tsiane suddenly roars, a deep animal sound which leaves him shuddering breathlessly but does not disconcert his patients. They watch impassively as he clutches his throat, trying to speak while apparently struggling to quell the lion that calls from fathomless depths. It is an awesome performance. Then Tsiane is abruptly restored to his former voice, continuing mid-sentence as if nothing unusual has happened.

He rings the bell and briefs a group of trainees, all of whom scramble into the pharmacy and begin preparing medicine, which smells much more pungent than the earlier preparations.

'This family wants to know if the young lady died naturally or if there was anything suspicious,' he explains. 'She died on 1st January and they came soon afterwards to see me. I told them, eight months ago, if there is witchcraft someone will speak. Now they are back to inform me that someone has spoken, an elderly woman, saying the mother-in-law killed her.

'This case concerns a big problem we have as traditional doctors: jealousy. Should someone work, someone be a genius, do something good, have a lot of money . . . there will be jealousy. The deceased's husband in this case is a successful businessman. He has a big house, he is wealthy: others will be jealous. The young lady, his wife, just said one day that she had a headache and a few minutes later she was dead.

'Yes, there was witchcraft in this case. I told them that. But in my practice, we don't disclose the identity of witches. I can do it. I know who they are but for the sake of my nation, I don't pinpoint witches. This is because I have done it before many times, when I was younger and inexperienced, but the result was always so sour. It doesn't pay any dividend to do it because all that happens is another person gets killed. Our people really do like to know who the witches are and sometimes, if you don't tell them, they will have suspicions and kill someone anyway, even if that person is not a witch. Many sangomas go after the witches and encourage these killings, but not me. I believe that if we teach people to point out witches, we're taking them to hell.

'So what I said here was: "The young lady died. She is gone

and you cannot get her back, no matter who you find to blame. Accept her death. Take the medicine we are giving you for protection against further witchcraft. Don't boast and show your money everywhere. Go quietly." '

Suddenly, there is a roar from one of the trainees in the dispensary. He appears in the interleading doorway on all-fours, panting and growling, spit running down his chin, looking imploringly at Tsiane.

The diviner shrugs. 'He's possessed. I was roaring myself before I became a sangoma. It is quite normal.'

* * *

The gulf between traditional and modern medicine remains wide but bridges are being built, sometimes unexpectedly. An Argentinian medical practitioner, Dr Gabriel Urgoiti, came to South Africa in 1981 and crossed the divide within days of arriving in Africa.

He was working in the busy casualty department of a township hospital in the province of Gauteng. One night when he was utterly exhausted, having been on duty for over twelve hours, Urgoiti saw a strange figure approaching. Tall and imposing in leopard skin and loin cloth, his dreadlocks entwined with bright beads, the man was holding a baby. Neither spoke much English and Urgoiti knew nothing about sangomas, but the two managed to understand each other.

Deducing from the mime that the man was a doctor of some exotic kind, Urgoiti could see at a glance that the baby was seriously ill. The patient was the sangoma's own child, Urgoiti realised, whose illness had not responded to traditional medicine. Knowing the one-year-old boy might be too sick to survive and hoping the sangoma would not blame him if the child died, Urgoiti reached for the baby, his eyes never leaving the healer's face for fear of causing offence.

A quick examination indicated the symptoms of meningitis, with little time left to act. In broken English, Urgoiti explained the lumbar puncture procedure and waited for the sangoma's consent. When the man nodded, Urgoiti invited him into the surgery to watch the test on the baby's spine.

Anxious about being observed by a medical man of vastly different experience, Urgoiti proceeded with extreme caution, the sangoma standing beside him, motionless. As soon as he saw the pus in the spinal fluid, Urgoiti knew his diagnosis was correct. The baby was dangerously ill. He explained his finding to the sangoma, who nodded and motioned the doctor to continue.

The baby was quickly admitted to the intensive care unit. Before going off duty, Urgoiti arranged for the sangoma to sleep at the hospital and then, waving the worried father farewell, he went home praying that the sangoma had understood his child might die or possibly suffer permanent brain damage.

Three weeks later, Urgoiti completed his final tests and told the sangoma that the little boy had made a complete recovery. Standing beside the cot while the healer dressed his wriggling son, Urgoiti watched as the father cut through an amulet the child had worn around his neck since birth. Handing it to Urgoiti, the sangoma said through an interpreter that, because western medicine had saved the boy, it was customary in Africa to award the child's life to the successful doctor.

Seven

Childhood Memory

The worldview of many modern Africans has been shaped by ancient religious and cultural beliefs absorbed in rural settings or urban slums. A survey conducted in July 1999 by the respected research organisation Population Communication Africa among Kenyan adolescent Aids orphans revealed that nearly 40 per cent believed their parents had died as a result of witchcraft.

Beliefs assimilated during childhood linger for ever, especially when they are comforting. In the past, childhood in Africa's eight hundred cultures bestowed universally beneficial characteristics, the most important of which was the psychological security fostered in traditional communities where customs were never doubted and life's opportunities seemed to be evenly distributed. Once perched precariously on the urban-rural divide in cities characterised by friction and scarcity, the ethnic morals taught to the young began to lose their grip. But, because they were not replaced by any new value system other than a scramble for goods, aspects of the old heritage persisted.

It is not hard to see why belief in the supernatural has endured. Witchcraft serves the useful function of providing victims of ever-present misfortune with an explanation when no other makes sense. In the case of the Aids orphans of Kenya, it provides an explanation as to why their parents suffered not one bout of sickness (which is understandable) but recurrent illnesses.

'Mother was a good and kind person,' one of the orphans told a researcher. 'A jealous co-wife cast a spell over mother so that she would fall from favour in father's eyes. This bewitching was the reason why mother lost her senses, caught cholera and died.'

Another teenager reported: 'Father and a neighbour quarrelled about a boundary fence. Father won the argument. But he was cursed by the neighbour and from that time on was always sick.'

Apart from their struggle to comprehend misfortune, most Africans continue to support kith and kin and to believe in some degree of communal rather than purely individual achievement. A person who gets ahead dramatically is still likely to stir the suspicions of neighbours, as illustrated by a favourite saying among the Bemba of Zambia: finding a beehive full of honey means good luck; finding two beehives is very good luck; finding three is witchcraft.

By acting as a check on undue individual effort, belief in the supernatural helps to sustain a rough egalitarianism. Though undoubtedly a source of many fears and much consequent misery, witchcraft also alleviates feelings of helplessness in abject circumstances.

Whatever its merits, magic has beguiled Africans since the continent's earliest inhabitants, facing tragic odds, first pinned their hopes on the supernatural. The following story by well-known African writer Camara Laye – who absorbed custom and superstition along with his breakfast porridge – illustrates the complexity of traditional beliefs. Describing childhood discovery in Guinea, West Africa, the story reveals the intensity with which Africans have learned their beliefs.

Traditional African societies, in observing rites of passage and ceremonies to mark the stages of life from birth to death, provide unambiguous definitions of what is expected of the individual. Ceremony provides the structure for celebrating the passage from one stage of life to the next, while ritual is the mechanism for keeping in touch with the spirit world.

The Dark Child by Camara Laye, reproduced here by kind permission of HarperCollins Publishers Limited, describes customary initiation rites experienced by the writer at the age of puberty. During the terrifying 'ceremony of the lions' he has to overcome his fear and show that he is ready to be entrusted with the secrets of manhood, including the knowledge that what he thought was the work of 'supernatural powers' during the initiation ceremony was in fact a drama created by the newly initiated young men in his community.

'I was growing up. The time had come for me to join the society of the uninitiated. This rather mysterious society – and at that age it was very mysterious to me, though not very secret – comprised all the young boys, all the uncircumcised, of twelve, thirteen and fourteen years of age, and it was run by our elders, whom we called the big Kondens. I joined it one evening before the feast of Ramadan.

As soon as the sun had gone down, the tom-tom had begun

to beat. Even though it was being played in a remote part of the concession, its notes had roused me at once, had struck my breast, had struck right at my heart, just as if Kodoke, our best player, had been playing for me alone. A little later I had heard the shrill voices of boys accompanying the tom-tom with their cries and singing. Yes, the time had come for me.

It was the first time I had spent the feast of Ramadan at Kouroussa. Until this year, my grandmother had always insisted on my spending it with her at Tindican. All that morning and even more so in the afternoon, I had been in a state of great agitation, with everyone busy preparing for the festival, bumping into and pushing each other and asking me to help. Outside, the uproar was just as bad. Kouroussa is the chief town of our region, and all the canton chiefs, attended by their musicians, make it a custom to gather here for the festival. From the gateway to the concession I had watched them pass by, with their companies of praise-singers, balaphonists and guitarists, drum and tom-tom players. Until now I had only been thinking of the festival and of the sumptuous feast that awaited me – but now there was something quite different in the wind.

The screaming crowd that surrounded Kodoke and his famous tom-toms was getting nearer. Going from one concession to another, the crowd would stop where there was a boy of an age to join the society, and take him away. That is why it was so slow in coming, yet so sure, so ineluctable. As sure, as ineluctable as the fate that awaited me.

What fate? My meeting with Konden Diara!

Now I was not aware of who Konden Diara was. My mother had often talked of him, and so at times had my uncles and whoever else had authority over me. They had threatened me only too often with Konden Diara, that terrible bogeyman, that "lion that eats up little boys". And here was Konden Diara – but was he man? Was he an animal? Was he not rather half-man, half-animal? My friend Kouyate believed he was more man than beast – here was Konden Diara leaving the dim world of hearsay, here he was taking on flesh and blood, yes, and roused by Kodoke's tom-tom was prowling around the town! This night was to be the night of Konden Diara.

Now I could hear the beating of the tom-tom very plainly – Kodoke was much nearer – I could hear perfectly the chanting and the shouts that rose into the dark. I could make out almost as distinctly the rather hollow, crisp, well-marked beats of the coros that are a kind of miniature canoe, and are beaten with a bit of wood. I was standing at the entrance to the concession, waiting. I, too, was holding my coro, ready to play it with the stick clutched nervously in my hand. I was waiting, hidden by the shadow of the hut. I was waiting, filled with a dreadful anxiety, my eyes searching the blackness.

"Well," asked my father. He had crossed the workshop without my hearing him. "Are you afraid?"

"A little," I replied.

He laid his hand on my shoulder. "It's alright. Don't worry." He drew me to him, and I could feel his warmth; it warmed me, too, and I began to feel less frightened; my heart did not beat so fast. "You mustn't be afraid."

"No."

I knew that whatever my fear might be I must be brave. I wasn't to show fright or to run off and hide. Still less was I to resist or cry out when my elders carried me off.

"I, too, went through this test," said my father.

"What happens to you," I asked.

"Nothing you need really be afraid of, nothing you can not overcome by your own willpower. Remember: you have to control your fear; you have to control yourself. Konden Diara will not take you away. He will roar. But he won't do more than roar. You won't be frightened, now, will you?"

"I'll try not to be."

"Even if you are frightened, do not show it."

He went away, and I began waiting again, and the disturbing uproar came nearer and nearer. Suddenly I saw the crowd emerging from the dark and rushing towards me. Kodoke, his tom-tom slung over one shoulder, was marching at their head, followed by the drummers.

I ran back quickly into the yard, and, standing in the middle of it, I awaited the awful invasion with as much courage as I could manage. I did not have long to wait. The crowd was upon me. It was spreading tumultuously all around me, overwhelming me with shouts and cries and beating tom-toms, beating drums. It formed a circle, and I found myself in the centre, alone, curiously isolated, still free and yet already captive. Inside the circle, I recognised Kouyate and others, many of them friends of mine who had been collected as the crowd moved on, collected as I was to be, as I already was; and it seemed to me that they were none of them looking very happy – but was I any more happy than they? I began to beat my coro, as they were doing. Perhaps I was beating it with less confidence than they.

At this point young girls and women joined the circle and began to dance; young men and adolescents, stepping out of the crowd, moved into the circle too and began to dance facing the women. The men sang, the women clapped their hands. Soon the only ones left to form the circle were the uncircumcised boys. They too began to sing – they were not allowed to dance – and, as they sang, sang in unison, they forgot their anxiety. I too sang with them. When, having formed a circle again, the crowd left our concession, I went with it, almost willingly, beating my coro with great enthusiasm. Kouyate was on my right.

Toward the middle of the night our tour of the town and the collection of uncircumcised boys were finished. We had arrived at the farthest outskirts of the concessions, and in front of us lay only the bush. Here the women and young girls left us. Then the grown men left. We were alone with the older boys, or should I say "delivered over" to them – for I remember the often rather disagreeable natures and rarely pleasant manners of those older ones.

The women and young girls now hurried back to their dwellings. Actually, they can not have been any more at ease than we were. I know for a fact that not one of them would have ventured to leave town on this night. Already, they found the town and the night sinister. I am certain that more than one who went back to her concession alone was to regret having joined the crowd. They took courage only after they had shut the gates of their concessions and the doors of their huts. Meanwhile, they hurried on and from time to time cast unquiet looks behind them. In a short while, when Konden Diara would begin to roar, they would not be able to stop shaking with fright; they would all shake uncontrollably. Then they would run to make sure the doors were all properly barred. For them, as for us, though in a much less significant way, this night would be the night of Konden Diara.

As soon as our elders had made sure that no intruder was present to disturb the mysteriousness of the ceremony, we left the town behind and entered the bush by a path which leads to a sacred place where each year the initiation takes place. The place is well known: it is situated under an enormous bombax tree, a hollow at the junction of the river Komoni and the river Niger. At normal times it is not forbidden to go there; but certainly it has not always been so, and some emanation from the past I never knew still seems to hover around the huge trunk of the bombax tree. I think that a night such as the one we were going through must certainly have resurrected a part of that past.

We were walking in silence, closely hemmed in by our elders. Perhaps they were afraid we might escape? It looked like it. I do not think, however, that the idea of escape had occurred to any of us. The night, and that particular night, seemed impenetrable. Who knew where Konden Diara had his lair? Who knew where he was prowling? But was it not right here, near the hollow? Yes, it must be here. And if we had to face him – and certainly we had to face him – it would surely be better to do so in a crowd, in this jostling group that seemed to make us all one, and seemed like a last refuge from the peril that was approaching.

Yet for all our nearness to one another and for all the vigilance of our elders, our march – so silent after the recent uproar – through the wan moonlight, far from the town, frightened us. And we were filled with terror at the thought of the sacred place toward which we were going, and the hidden presence of Konden Diara.

Were our elders marching so closely behind us only to keep watch over us? Perhaps. But it is likely that they too felt something of the terror which had seized us. They too found the night and the silence disturbing. And for them, as for us, marching close together was a means of allaying terror.

Just before we reached the hollow we saw flames leap from

a huge wood fire previously hidden by bushes. Kouyate squeezed my arm, and I knew he was referring to the fire. Yes, there was a fire. There too was Konden Diara, the hidden presence of Konden Diara. But there was also a reassuring in the depth of the night: a great fire! My spirits rose – at least they rose a little – and I squeezed Kouyate's arm in return. I quickened my steps – we all quickened our steps – and the crimson radiance of the fire enveloped us. We had a harbour now, this kind of haven from the night: a huge blaze, and, at our backs, the enormous trunk of the bombax tree. Oh! It was a precarious haven! But, however poor, it was infinitely better than the silence and the dark, the sullen silence of the dark. We assembled beneath the bombax tree. The ground beneath had been cleared of reeds and tall grasses.

Our elders suddenly shouted: "Kneel!" We at once fell to our knees.

"Heads down!" We lowered our heads.

"Lower than that!" We bent our heads right to the ground, as if in prayer.

"Now hide your eyes!"

We didn't have to be told twice. We shut our eyes tight and pressed our hands over them. For would we not die of fright and horror if we should see, or so much as catch a glimpse of Konden Diara? Our elders walked up and down, behind us and in front of us, to make sure that we had all obeyed their orders to the letter. Woe to him who would have the audacity to disobey! He would be cruelly whipped. It would be a whipping all the more cruel because he would have no hope of redress, for he would find no one to listen to his complaint, no one to transgress against custom. But who would have the audacity to disobey?

Now that we were on our knees with our foreheads to the ground and our hands pressed over our eyes, Konden Diara's roaring suddenly burst out.

We were expecting to hear this hoarse roar, we were not expecting any other sound, but it took us by surprise and shattered us, froze our hearts with its unexpectedness. And it was not only a lion, it was not only Konden Diara roaring: there were ten, twenty, perhaps thirty lions that took their lead from him, uttering their terrible roars and surrounding the hollow; ten or twenty lions separated from us by a few yards only and whom the great wood fire would perhaps not always keep at bay; lions of every size and every age – we could tell that by the way they roared – from the very oldest ones to the very youngest cubs. No, not one of us would dream of venturing to open an eye, not one! Not one of us would dare to lift his head from the ground; he would rather bury it in the earth. And I bent down as far as I could; we all bent down further; we bent our knees as much as we could; we kept our backs as low as possible. I made myself – we all made ourselves – as small as we could.

"You mustn't be afraid," I said to myself. "You must master your fear! Your father has commanded you to!"

But how was I to master it? Even in the town, far away from this clearing, women and children trembled and hid themselves in their huts. They heard the growling of Konden Diara, and many of them stopped their ears to keep it out. The braver arose – that night it took courage to leave one's bed – and went again and again to check the doors and see that they were shut tight. How was I to stave off fear when I was within range of the dread monster? If he pleased, Konden Diara could leap the fire in one bound and sink his claws in my back!

I did not doubt the presence of the monster, not for a single instant. Who could assemble such a numerous herd, hold such a nocturnal revel, if not Konden Diara?

"He alone," I said to myself, "he alone has such power over lions . . . Keep away, Konden Diara! Keep away! Go back into the bush! . . ." But Konden Diara went on with his revels, and sometimes it seemed to me that he roared right over my head, right into my own ears. "Keep away, I implore you, Konden Diara!"

What was it my father had said? "Konden Diara roars; but he won't do more than roar; he will not take you away . . ." Yes, something like that. But was it true, really true?

There was also a rumour that Konden Diara sometimes pounced with fearsome claws on someone or other and carried him far away, far, far away into the depths of the bush; and then, days and days afterwards, months or even years later, quite by chance a huntsman might discover some whitened bones.

And do people also die of fright? Ah! How I wished this roaring would stop! How I wished I was far away from this clearing, back in the concession, in the warm security of the hut! Would this roaring never cease?

"Go away, Konden Diara! Go away! Stop roaring." Oh! Those roars! I felt as if I could bear them no longer.

Whereupon, suddenly, they stopped! They stopped just as they had begun, so suddenly, in fact, that I felt only reluctant relief. Was it over? Really over? Was it not just a temporary interruption? No, I dared not feel relieved just yet. And then suddenly the voice of one of the older boys rang out: "Get up!"

I heaved a sigh of relief. This time it was really over. We

looked at one another: I looked at Kouyate and the others. If there were only a little more light . . . Yes, we were afraid. We were not able to conceal our fear.

A new command rang out, and we sat down in front of the fire. Now our elders began our initiation. For the rest of the night they taught us the chants sung by the uncircumcised. We never moved. We learned the words and tunes as we heard them. We were attentive as if we had been at school, entirely attentive and docile.

When dawn came, our instruction was at an end. My legs and arms were numb. I worked my joints and rubbed my legs for a while, but my blood still flowed slowly. I was worn out, and I was cold. Looking around me, I could not understand why I had shaken with fear during the night: the first rays of dawn were falling so gently, so reassuringly, on the bombax tree, on the clearing. The sky looked so pure! Who would have believed that a few hours earlier a pack of lions led by Konden Diara in person had been raging fiercely in the high grass and among the reeds, and that they had been separated from us only by a wood fire which had just now gone out as dawn came? No one. I would have doubted my own senses and set it all down as a nightmare if I had not noticed more than one of my companions casting an occasional fearful glance in the direction of the highest grass.

But what were those long white threads which hung from, or, rather, waved from the top of the bombax tree and which appeared to write on the sky the direction in which the town lay? I had not time to wonder very long at this: our elders were regrouping us; and, because most of us were almost sleep-walking, the operation was carried out with difficulty, with shouts, and with some rough treatment. Finally we started off back to the town, singing our new songs, and we sang them with unbelievably carefree abandon: as the steed that scents the approaching stable suddenly quickens his step, however weary he may be.

When we reached the first concession, the presence of the long white threads struck me once more: all the principal huts had those threads on the very tops of their roofs.

"Do you see the white threads?" I asked Kouyate.

"I can see them. They are always there after the ceremony in the clearing."

"Who puts them there?"

Kouyate shrugged his shoulders.

"That's where they come from," I said, pointing to the distant bombax tree.

"Someone must have climbed up."

"Who could possibly climb a bombax tree?"

"I don't know."

"Could anyone possibly get his arms around such a huge trunk?" I said. "And even if he could, how could he hoist himself on bark all covered with all those thorns? You're talking nonsense. Can't you imagine what a job it would be just to reach the first branches?"

"Why do you expect me to know more about this than you do?" asked Kouyate.

"Because this is the first time I have taken part in the ceremony, while you . . ."

I didn't finish my sentence. We had reached the main square

of the town. I stared in amazement at the bombax trees in the market place. They too were ornamented with the same white threads. All but the humblest huts, indeed, and all the big trees were tied to one another by these white threads whose focal point was the enormous bombax tree in the clearing, the sacred place marked by the bombax tree.

“The swallows tie them on,” said Kouyate suddenly.

“Swallows? Are you crazy?” I said. “Swallows don’t fly by night.”

I questioned one of the older boys who was walking beside me.

“It is our great chief who does it,” he said. “Our chief turns himself into a swallow during the night. He flies from tree to tree and from hut to hut, and all these threads are tied on in less time than it takes to tell.”

“He flies from tree to tree like a swallow?”

“Yes, he’s a real swallow and as swift. Everyone knows that.”

“Isn’t that what I told you?” asked Kouyate.

I did not say another word. The night of Konden Diara was a strange night, a terrible and miraculous night, a night that passed all understanding.

As on the previous evening, we went from one concession to another, preceded by tom-toms and drums, and our companions left us one after another as they reached their homes. Whenever we passed a concession where someone whose courage had failed him had refused to join us, a mocking chant rose from our ranks.

I arrived at our concession completely exhausted but very satisfied with myself: I had taken part in the ceremony of the lions! Even if I had not put up much of a show when Konden Diara was roaring, that was my own affair; I could keep that to myself. I passed triumphantly over the threshold of our concession.

The festival of Ramadan was beginning. In the yard, I saw my parents, who were dressed to go to the mosque.

"Here you are at last," said my mother.

"Here I am," I said proudly.

"What kind of time is this to come home?" she said, pressing me to her bosom. "The night is over, and you haven't had a bit of sleep."

"The ceremony did not finish until break of day," I said.

"I know, I know," she said. "All you men are mad."

"What about the lions?" asked my father. "What about Konden Diara?"

"I heard them," I replied. "They were very close; they were as near to me as I am to you now. There was only the fire between us."

"It's crazy," said my mother. "Go to bed, you're dropping with sleep." She turned to my father: "Now, where's the sense in all that?"

"Well, it's the custom," said my father.

"I don't like such customs," she said. "Young boys should not have to stay awake all night."

"Were you afraid?" asked my father.

Should I admit that I was frightened?

"Of course he was afraid," said my mother.

"Only a little," said my father.

"Go to bed," ordered my mother. "If you don't get some sleep now you'll fall asleep during the feast."

I went inside to lie down. Outside I heard my mother quarrelling with my father. She thought it stupid to take unnecessary risks.

Later I got to know who Konden Diara was, and I learned these things when the time had come for me to learn them. As long as we are not circumcised, as long as we have not attained that second life that is our true existence, we are told nothing, and we can find out nothing.

We begin to have a vague understanding of the ceremony of the lions after we have taken part in it many times. But even then, we are careful to share our knowledge only with those companions who have had the same experience. And the real secret lies hidden until the day when we are initiated into our life as men.

No, they were not real lions that roared in the clearing, for it was the older boys, simply the older boys. They created the roaring sound with small boards, thick at the centre, sharp at the edges: the edges were all sharper for having such a thick centre. The board was ellipsoidal in shape and very small. There was a hole on one side that permitted it to be tied to a string. The older boys swung it around like a sling, and, to increase the speed of the gyrations, they too turned with it. The board cut through the air and produced a sound like a lion's roar. The smallest board imitated the roaring of the lion cubs; the biggest ones the roaring of full-grown lions.

It was childishly simple. What was not so childish was the effect produced at night on someone who did not expect it: the heart froze! If it had not been for the far greater fear of finding themselves lost in the bush, the terror it created would have made the boys run away. The bombax tree and the fire which had been kindled near it made a kind of haven which kept the uninitiated from running away.

But if Konden Diara's roaring is easily explained, the presence of the long white threads binding the great bombax tree in the sacred clearing, to the tallest trees and the principal houses in the town, is less easily explained. For my own part, I never succeeded in obtaining an explanation: at the time when I might have obtained it, that is, when I should have taken my place among the older boys who conducted the ceremony, I was no longer living at Kouroussa. All I know is that these threads were spun from cotton and that bamboo poles were used to tie them to the tops of the huts. What I don't know is how they were attached to the tops of the bombax trees.

Our bombax trees are very big, and it is difficult to imagine poles sixty feet high. Such structures would certainly collapse, no matter how carefully they had been put together. Moreover, I do not see how the summit of those thorny trees could be reached by climbing. There is of course a kind of belt which tree-climbers use. It is tied around the tree and the climber gets inside it, placing the belt against the small of his back, then climbs by a series of jerks, pressing against the trunk with his feet. But such a procedure is quite preposterous given the enormous size of the trunks of our bombax trees.

Or why not plainly and simply use a sling? I do not know. A good slinger can work miracles. Perhaps it is this sort of miracle which would most easily explain the inexplicable presence of white threads at the summit of the bombax trees. But I can come to no final decision about it.

I do know that the men who tie the threads to the rooftops have to take great care not to mislay the bamboo poles. Things must not be revealed in that fashion. For it would take only one mislaid pole to start the women and children on the way to discovering the secret. That is why, as soon as the threads are untied, the poles and boards are removed. The usual hideouts are thatched roofs and secret places in the bush. And so nothing escapes about these manifestations of the power of Konden Diara.

But what about the men? What about those who *do* know?

They won't breathe a single word about it. They keep their knowledge a close secret. Not only do they keep women and children in a state of uncertainty and terror, they also warn them to keep the doors of their huts firmly barred.

I know that such conduct might appear strange, but it is absolutely true. If the ceremony of the lions has the character of a game, if it is for the most part pure mystification, yet it has one important feature: it is a test, a training in hardship, a rite; the prelude to a tribal rite, and for the present that is all one can say . . . It is obvious that if the secret were to be given away, the ceremony would lose much of its power.

Certainly the teaching which follows the roaring of Konden Diara would remain the same. But nothing would remain of the trial by fear, that occasion when every boy has the opportunity to overcome his fear and his own baser nature. Nothing would remain of the necessary preparation for the painful tribal rite of circumcision. But, at the moment of writing this, does any part of the rite still survive? The secret . . . Do we still have secrets?'

Eight

The Milingo Affair

Emmanuel Milingo had been a controversial Roman Catholic priest in Zambia for years before his name hit the international headlines. But in 1982, a story in American *Newsweek* titled 'The Vatican's Medicine-Man' signalled his role in a dramatic clash between Rome and traditional Africa.

Newsweek described Milingo's use of 'rattles and charms', while *Der Spiegel* in Germany reported that his holy ministrations relied on such 'pagan instruments as cow-dung, cockroaches and chicken bones'.

Zambian-born Emmanuel Milingo's turbulent tenure began when he returned to his country from studying in Ireland in 1969 to learn to his great surprise that he had been appointed Roman Catholic Archbishop of Lusaka at the age of thirty-nine. The archdiocese had hitherto been run by white missionaries along strictly conventional lines, and Milingo took his election as an indication that Africans were now expected to make their own contribution to the Church's life.

He immediately began Africanising the liturgy, introducing drums during services and forming a choir dressed in traditional Zambian costume to accompany him on confirmation tours in the archdiocese. Believing that Christian spirituality should be lived in a concrete human condition, he founded a congregation called Daughters of the Redeemer to demonstrate that Catholics were specifically Zambian. They wore the *chitenge*, a traditional wraparound cloth, instead of the nun's habit – much to the alarm of Milingo's white colleagues.

Undeterred by the disquiet stirred by his independent instincts, Milingo caused further unease in his Easter Message of 1970 by publicly criticising the Church's collaboration with the racist Portuguese rulers of Angola and Mozambique. Saying that Catholics were perpetuating 'evils' in Africa, he went on the following year to condemn the Zambian government's legalisation of abortion as 'baby butchery'. The state responded swiftly, accusing Milingo of 'cheap sentimentalism and sensational religious propaganda'. He was summoned to Rome and rebuked by the Vatican's Secretariat of State.

Archbishop Milingo's main concern was to restore African self-esteem. 'The inferiority complex which haunts Africa in relation with Europe,' he wrote, 'is a perpetual humiliation which has come about by the historical colonialism in politics, economics and religion. I have added religion because religion in its subtle ways does not attribute to itself the pains it causes to those it submits to itself.'

Despite Rome's censure, Milingo continued to express his

social convictions in public, increasing his popularity among Zambians but damaging his reputation with the Church and the government.

By 1973, he had turned his attention to the sick. Instinctively a pastoral priest, he believed the Church's task was to care for all who were in need, whether or not they were Christians. His guiding principles were inspiration in the Lord and in the dignity of Africa. According to Gerrie ter Haar in her biography of Milingo, *Spirit of Africa*, Milingo felt a deep responsibility for the sanctity of African religion as the only area of life where Africans had retained their own identity.

In April that year, a sick woman came to Milingo for help, an event he described as a turning point in his life.

> She sometimes could spend months on end without eating anything. She could only drink water or soft drinks. She feared her child because she did not consider him a human being. She constantly heard voices speaking to her. She was treated at a mental hospital, but to no avail. On the 2nd April 1973 she came to my office. She explained her problem. I told her we should pray together. She came back . . . and once more explained everything systematically to me. I brought her to my residence where I heard her Confession, then we celebrated Mass. But in spite of all this, the voices continued to be heard and she still feared her own child. At that time I did not know how Satan behaves once he is in possession of someone. I contemplated various ways of helping the woman, when suddenly an idea glowed in my mind: 'Look three times intently into her eyes and ask her to look three times intently into yours. Tell her to close her eyes the third time and order her to sleep. Then speak to her soul after signing her with the sign of the cross.'
>
> I carried out this instruction systematically. The woman was overshadowed by the power of the Lord. She relaxed calmly and so I was able to reach her soul. I prayed as much as I could, then I woke her up. We both did not know what had happened to us.

Milingo later explained that 'the Lord was leading me to the healing of the disease that is common among people, *mashawe* (spirit possession). This disease cannot be treated in a hospital.' He believed the power of the Holy Spirit had overcome the evil forces which had taken possession of the woman and made her ill. The woman herself, believing she had been exorcised of the evil spirits, made a complete recovery.

Archbishop Milingo viewed his encounter with the possessed woman as a holy revelation and proceeded to plan a healing ministry. In his search for understanding of *mashawe*, he talked to village elders and traditional healers, becoming convinced not only of the prevalence of the disease but also of his ability to help the thousands of people who suffered from it.

Once convinced, he made a public declaration:

> Brethren, we have for a very long time suffered from *mashawe*, and we have had to find the doctors outside our own Church. We can heal this disease in our own Catholic Church. So, if any of you suffer from this disease, let them come forward and we shall try to help them.

Milingo's new ministry was based on Africa's belief in what he called 'the world in between' – a spirit world located between the kingdom of God and the realm of humankind; a world which included ancestral and other protective spirits but was also the abode of evil spirits.

Milingo understood that Zambians' perception of illness included African spiritual, mythical and physical concepts. The Catholic Church, meanwhile, felt threatened by what it saw as pagan-Christian theology openly embraced by one of its senior clerics, and believed it had to secure its doctrine against infringement. In announcing his new healing ministry, Archbishop Milingo had launched himself on a collision course with the Vatican.

Word of Milingo's healing gift spread rapidly throughout Zambia. People who believed they were suffering from *mashawe* began to arrive in droves at his church services, his office and his residence. Milingo documented some of his important recovery cases, writing of the extraordinary powers of his right hand in communicating 'healing radiations'.

He longed to discuss his new ministry with theologians, other than those in Zambia who were mainly opposed to his methods. Not yet familiar with charismatic developments abroad, he attended a seminar of the Better World Movement near Rome, where he was warmly received and began a close study of the Second Vatican Council. While reading in his bed one night, he saw a shadow approaching, which then covered him until he was in 'a state of transformation'. A voice told him: 'Go and preach the gospel', from which he deduced that he should conduct his healing ministry within the Church. 'Otherwise the voice would have told me, "Go and heal the sick," ' he explained.

After his return to Zambia, Milingo received a letter from the Vatican urging him to stop healing. Surprised by the speed of this injunction, he complained that 'while I was still trying to understand what had befallen on me, some people had already written to Rome and had declared that what I was doing was evil'.

Milingo was offended that the Vatican had not bothered to send a delegate to Lusaka to gather first-hand evidence, yet he decided he must comply with Rome's instruction by ignoring those suffering from *mashawe*. But crowds of people continued to follow him everywhere. His residence became a public place, always crammed with sick Zambians as well as ailing people from neighbouring countries.

Tormented at having to spurn the sick, Milingo decided to address the local clergy on the matter. The night before his meeting with the Church, he had another dream. 'The Lord Jesus said to me: "If they do not believe that the powers you have are God-given, you should take an egg, hold it for a time in your right hand till it warms up. You then break it open and out of it will come a chicken." ' Milingo wondered if the dream meant that it was sometimes necessary to do things that were contrary to the laws of nature in order to convince doubters.

The next morning, a woman who said she had suffered for ten years from *mashawe* came to see him. He explained that he did not have permission to heal her, but the woman refused to go away. She told him she had already lost three husbands because of her illness: Milingo was her last resort.

Milingo said later:

> Up until then I had not grasped the meaning of the dream, but then suddenly I did. The Lord brought the sick woman while the case-hearings were on. Without much reflection I brought the woman with me to the meeting. After I had spoken to the priests for some time, I called her and healed her in the sight of all. Some were astonished and wondered. Some jeered, others mocked. There was not one diocesan priest who stood up to defend me. I left the place completely disappointed and demoralised.

The Church's subsequent investigation into the Archbishop's healing powers concluded that they were natural rather than spiritual – and incorporated hypnotism. Milingo was devastated.

> I felt so ashamed before my Church that I had nowhere to hide my head . . . I thought that our prayer was more powerful than

> the prayer of the traditional religion and, indeed, I still believe so, even if the missionaries made no effort to understand religious problems of our people and prefer to misjudge this method of incarnating Christ into the soul of an African.

Milingo tried to comply with Rome's ban but the struggle proved too great. Resignedly, he resumed his healing ministry because he simply could not avoid the sick, a fact that became obvious even to his harshest critics in the Church. He also continued criticising Zambia's elite as 'showy, urban educated fools'. Quick to point out that Africa's new political leaders were no different from their old colonial masters, he observed: 'One is surprised how suddenly a good and simple Christian of yesterday changes into a brute when he is drunk with power and wealth.'

Invited to address a meeting by a charismatic movement in Ann Arbor, Michigan in 1976, Milingo at last found moral and spiritual support. While among his theological admirers, the Archbishop received a divine message through a vision which came to him at Ann Arbor. 'You will still have to suffer,' it said, 'but you will come out of it.'

On his return to Zambia, Milingo initiated a number of charismatic groups within the archdiocese of Lusaka to provide a structural base for his healing ministry. But his charismatic connections only exacerbated conflict with the Church. While Rome tolerated the expatriate charismatic version already practised in Zambia among Irish Catholics – using charismata (gifts of the Holy Spirit) for renewal – it feared Milingo's inclusion of African spirits residing in his 'world in between'. The Irish priests were unfamiliar with *mashawe* and aghast at its outward manifestations – convulsions, frothing at the mouth, howling and animal roaring. Unable to identify with Milingo's work, they dismissed *mashawe* as hysteria. Inexorably, the 'world in between' loomed as a fraught test-case in Rome.

Milingo's support within the worldwide charismatic movement meant he could neither be ignored nor overtly disciplined. His integrity and determination meant he could not be bullied into submission. The Archbishop's Christian credentials were beyond reproach, his actions always having been based on the wisdom of the Bible, periodically strengthened by visions along the lines of the Old Testament prophets.

Milingo continued to explore the concept of 'inculturation' which featured prominently in the Second Vatican Council. He was convinced that for Christianity to become firmly implanted in Africa, it had to take root within African culture. But his idea of Africanisation went far beyond the interpretation of the local missionaries – and of the Vatican. Although Milingo was looking for ways to bring the Church closer to the people and into their lives, as Vatican II decreed, his methods were an embarrassment to Rome.

While on a visit to France, Milingo was called upon to heal Theresa Gacambi, Mother-General of the Assumption Sisters in Nairobi, Kenya, who had been seriously injured in a car crash three years earlier. The accident had left her with a maimed hand, one leg shorter than the other, and much pain. Milingo wrote:

> I consulted the Lord in order to have a glimpse of the brokenness of Mother Gacambi. I am grateful to the Lord, my request was answered. I was shown how like a patched clay pot was her body. I also understood the condition of her hands and legs . . . When I met her, I introduced the matter. I had reproduced in a poor picture what I experienced in a mental picture of her situation. I had drawn the picture as far as I could, since I am not an artist. She confirmed what I said and what I had drawn on a picture.

After two sessions of prayer, Mother Gacambi announced

that she was healed, a claim confirmed by her medical doctor.

Milingo was again advised to stop healing by the Zambian Episcopal Conference in 1977, but he felt powerless to overlook the sick who constantly besieged him. By the end of 1978, however, the numbers requesting his help were so great that he believed the situation to be beyond his control. By now, his own staff feared the consequences of abandoning the healing ministry. Yet the Church persisted in its condemnation.

Eventually, Milingo abandoned the unequal battle, publicly announcing that:

> . . . it was never my intention to work outside the Church of Rome, nor the local Church in Zambia. It has never been my intention to look extraordinary, nor to call for admiration. I came into the healing ministry by a pure love from Jesus Christ, who gave the gift of healing, not of right, but by favour and privilege. Hence, since I want to remain a faithful servant of the Catholic Church universal and local, may you all know that I have decided to follow the advice of the Bishops. My last public healing session therefore will be on 25th February, 1979.

The Bishops were furious that Milingo had publicly blamed them for ending his healing ministry. Their indignation soared as they observed his final healing session, attended by so many people that it had to be held outside the cathedral. The event was widely reported in the local media, which had always been sympathetic to Milingo, not only in respect of his healing work but also for his outspoken commentary on social and political injustices in Zambia.

In a letter to the Vatican, protesting against the Bishops' accusation that he had caused 'scandal and division' within his diocese, Milingo described his final healing session.

> This time the number was tripled . . . The exact number will be soon out, since the news media were present. As we finished praying we went on to bless holy water, which they take home. There were buckets of water, which they cherished so much on this day, as they knew that both the priests who were conducting weekly sessions and myself have been forbidden to carry on healing. As I gave them my last blessing, they took hold of me, struggling to kiss my hand, to touch me or to be blessed. I had to be protected and led to the car. As I was in the car someone knelt at my side-door and wept bitterly, and another asked to go with me, but the elders who always accompany me in healing sessions took them away.

Because the demand for his healing continued unabated, Milingo tried initially to write letters to the thousands of people who sought his help. But by the end of 1979, he wrote in despair to the Vatican:

> I am terribly harassed by people, at home, at my office, through letters and telephones. They have never learnt to obey. The Bishops must speak openly to them under obedience not to come to me. How I long to lead a normal life again. If you can allow me to abscond from my house, and carry out my administrative duties from somewhere, I shall appreciate your advice. What a mental torture to learn to be hard and harsh to the sick by your orders, and this is what I am trying to learn. But in spite of this they are coming, coming, coming . . .

To the fury of the Bishops, demonstrations broke out in Lusaka in support of Milingo's banned ministry. On the occasion of the Archbishop's fiftieth birthday celebration in Kabwe, arranged to coincide with a confirmation, Milingo recognised the risk of provoking the Church and warned the congregation to sit while calling upon the Holy Spirit because '. . . when we call upon the Holy Spirit to come, He really does come. He comes with power.' But the congregation did not heed his caution and proceeded to demonstrate their spirit possession by falling down, screaming and jerking. The cathedral erupted in the chaotic way the Bishops found repulsive, and Milingo was accused of breaking his promise.

Demonstrations continued. Milingo retreated to stay with the Daughters of the Redeemer at Mount Zion while the Vatican investigated his alleged breach of trust. After travelling to the United States for an international charismatic conference, he went to Rome for a meeting with Pope John Paul II, before returning to Lusaka – and yet another crisis.

One of the Daughters, Sister Catherine Kaimfa, had been on a three-month course in Kenya. When she returned, her fellow sisters believed she was pregnant because she had gained a lot of weight. Milingo, informed of this suspicion by the Daughters, decided that the only way to stop the rumours was a medical examination. Sister Catherine at first objected, but then agreed. The diagnosis revealed she was not pregnant, but needed an operation for a medical complaint associated with her weight gain. However, subsequent examinations indicated she did not need the surgical procedure after all.

A few days later, Milingo was informed by the Church of a rumour that Sister Catherine was not only pregnant but that the cause of her pregnancy was the Archbishop himself, who was alleged to be trying to conceal his guilt through a secret abortion. Refusing to accept the findings of the previous medical examinations, the Bishops demanded another by a doctor of their choice.

Sister Catherine refused. Only after Milingo begged her did she go for the final examination. The results were again negative.

At Easter in 1982, Milingo received a letter from the Church requesting him to go to Rome as soon as possible 'for a certain period (of) theological studies and quiet reflection, as well as to seek medical advice from the doctors'.

Milingo departed, a sad man leaving the mystified people of Zambia behind him. 'The unthinkable, although not quite unexpected, has happened,' wrote the journal of Zambia's churches. 'Archbishop Milingo has been removed from his archdiocese for an indefinite period, and perhaps for good.' The Church offered no explanation when it appointed his temporary successor.

In Rome Milingo was isolated from the international media, which had become fascinated by the affair. He lodged with the Passionate Fathers in the centre of the city, entirely ignorant of his future and the popular campaigns being waged in Lusaka for his return. He was plied with learned works on the Holy Spirit, and was obliged to submit to extensive medical examinations arranged by the Vatican, despite having been pronounced medically fit after routine tests two years earlier, when the condition of his heart was described as 'that of a twenty-year-old'. After several psychological investigations, one of the consulting psychotherapists refused to pursue the matter further on the grounds that Milingo was completely sane.

The Archbishop again appealed to the Pope. 'Most Holy Father, release me, I want to go home,' he wrote. 'You are the Daniel in my case.'

A year later, by which time he had gradually gained more freedom in Rome, Milingo was finally granted an audience. 'Your bent,' said the Pope, 'is the healing ministry. Let us then discuss together what you can do in Rome.' The two apparently cut a deal, although Archbishop Milingo has never disclosed its exact terms.

Several weeks later, the Vatican accepted Milingo's resignation as Archbishop of Lusaka and appointed him a Special Delegate to the Pontifical Commission for Migration and Tourism. He was allowed to retain his episcopal dignity.

No mention was made in the official resignation announcement of Milingo's 'healing bent', but his routine in Rome ever since has been to spend the mornings in his office at the Vatican, while in the afternoons he freely dedicates himself to the sick, mainly Italians. Once a month he holds a public healing service in Rome, which is attended by large crowds from all over the world. Needless to say, few Africans come to Rome to see him.

Whatever the Church's objections to Milingo's healing ministry in an African context, they evidently did not apply in a western setting. The Milingo affair clearly revealed that the Roman Catholic hierarchy believed the Holy Spirit could speak only through its religious elite and only in their language – not in the language of Africa.

The language of metaphor permeates all religions, it being the imaginative statement of a different reality to the one we actually live. Metaphor provides the idealised image, while belief provides the power to transform the metaphor into reality. Emmanuel Milingo's healing right hand may not have been anything more than a metaphor but it offered his followers a better reality than the troubled one that had brought them together in the first place.

All forms of divination and healing – including that practised by the Catholic Church – search for different ways of knowing and different ways of restoring a world of social reciprocity. It is more than likely that Emmanuel Milingo, a man of exceptional wisdom and personal character, is better able to heal troubled Africans whose beliefs are rooted in traditional ideas than is anyone drilled in conventional western categorical thought and hailing from Rome. The best healers everywhere are those who are exceptionally well tuned to the psychological realm in which so many of humanity's problems lie.

Nine

Magical, Mystery Creatures

Fascinating figures haunt the soul of Africa, including sexual spirits that lurk beyond the taboos of society. In South Africa, the seductive *thokoloshe* and the *impundulu* have exploited erotic female passions for centuries, while a beautiful being called the *momlambo* is reputed to enslave even the most high-minded of men in her fleeting embrace.

Descriptions of the *thokoloshe* vary but he exists, in one guise or another, in the minds of people throughout Africa. He is a little man, never taller than one metre, with whom it is impossible to make eye contact. He has only one buttock and an extraordinarily long penis which he slings over his shoulder. Some believe he comes from the womb of a witch as a result of her copulation with a baboon; some that he is conjured up by witchcraft, or caught by sorcerers who lie in wait for him at night, keeping him a prisoner until he is indoctrinated as a familiar. The witch is said to use the *thokoloshe* as a sexual partner while he is undergoing training or when he is not representing her in the homes of her victims.

Some say he lives with the spirits under water. One of his favoured sports, like Pan from classical mythology, is seducing young girls who come unsuspectingly to his pool to bathe or wash their clothes. It is extremely unwise to have an affair with a *thokoloshe*, though he is a masterly lover, because you may have a disabled baby by him. Frigidity in a woman is claimed to be the work of a *thokoloshe* lover.

Many urban homes in Africa contain beds hoisted high on bricks as a defence against the *thokoloshe*'s amorous advances. Another precaution, which has been a mystery for decades to white employers whose domestic staff implore them to bring bottles of sea water back from coastal holidays, is to sprinkle the water on the outside walls of the house in the belief that the *thokoloshe* will smell the salt and be fooled into thinking that he will have to cross an ocean in order to invade.

Menacing creatures like the *thokoloshe* usually torment those who are in a temporary delusional state, often drug-induced or symptomatic of a psychosis like schizophrenia. Africans suffering from a common illness known by many names – such as *uthukwase* in South Africa or *mashawe* in Zambia – exist in a kind of self-hypnosis, believing they are possessed by spirits that swirl in pools and rivers. Such hallucinations leap forth, often in the form of mythical creatures, when barriers surrounding forbidden regions of the mind disappear as a result of drugs, mental illness or religious fervour.

The *thokoloshe* is a dwarf; his head unusually large for his body; his short, muscular arms and legs out of proportion to his torso. He wears a soft sheepskin kaross, tied above his left shoulder, which conceals his giant phallus. In his right hand, he carries a fighting stick to conquer foes. It is only when he is going to seduce a woman that he pulls the kaross to the right across his bare chest and exposes his awesome penis. Women who have had a sexual encounter with him are said to remain in a state of erotic excitement for days afterwards. This is because it is not only the manner of his lovemaking that makes the experience unforgettable, but also the powerful magic he employs to ensure that his lovers' senses are attuned solely to the pleasure of sex.

The mythology of the *thokoloshe*, with his powerful sex drive and outsized phallus, probably originated in a primordial period when the male sexual instinct was revered as the source of procreation – possibly during a time of struggle between the matriarchal and patriarchal cultures in Africa.

In southern Africa, the *thokoloshe* lives mainly in water, although some say he is a miner like one of Snow White's dwarfs who digs by day for precious metals. According to a Zulu sangoma: 'He is not good or bad. He cannot do anything except what men tell him. Men are wicked, so he is wicked, but children can play with him and he is good to them.'

When he appears, the *thokoloshe* causes mayhem along the lines of poltergeist phenomena: things fall down, knock, curdle, collide and disappear. As a precaution against his invasion, the Zulu sangoma recommends:

> Wear snakeskin round the wrist. If you do not wish to look superstitious, get a snakeskin strap for your watch. A man should give him a bowl of blood. That satisfies him. For a woman it is perhaps best to let him sleep with her. But she must be careful, for he can steal her spirit.
>
> Get him on your side . . . He can make life hell. He chokes

> you, dances on the roof, sleeps with your girl, sets the room afire – anything. He turns into shapes. He wakes you every time you fall asleep. And if he says, 'do this', you do it because he is much stronger than you are.

The *thokoloshe* takes the blame for many crimes in Africa. 'It was not my wish to murder,' stated the defendant in one South African trial. 'But there was the *thokoloshe*. The *thokoloshe* nipped me and said, "Kill!", and I killed.' As an extenuating circumstance, the *thokoloshe* is to African courts what the failed memory ('everything went blank') is to puzzled jurors elsewhere.

The *thokoloshe* is a creature whose unbounded promiscuity is countered by his benign image as a trickster adored by children, whereas the *impundulu* is altogether evil. Associated with witchcraft and noted for a peculiar form of sexual gratification which women find irresistible, he is said to have a kick so devastating that it causes the victim to cough blood. (Those who report this curse are often found to be suffering from tuberculosis.)

While the *thokoloshe* engages in conventional coitus, the *impundulu*'s phallus is a thick, flat, tongue-like organ used in a sexual act similar to cunnilingus. He is a bird resembling a young ostrich in size, with gorgeously soft, velvety feathers which rate highly among Africa's most powerful forms of love magic. If a woman's body is stroked with an *impundulu* feather, her senses are set alight. But those who find gratification from the *impundulu* ultimately lose their minds.

It is said that a woman who secretly has a sexual relationship with the *impundulu* will subsequently marry a man in accordance with custom, but will always lack a normal sexual response. Cold and indifferent, she will yield only because she has no choice.

Perhaps this myth has its origin in an archaic period when conception was attributed to a supernatural power symbolised by a bird. The advent of patriarchal rule and the phallic cult might have relegated a once sacred primeval creature like the *impundulu*, which seems to have been associated with virgin births and possibly lesbianism, to the loathsome status of a bloodthirsty seducer of women: a fallen icon, like Lucifer.

At any rate, the *impundulu*'s sexual behaviour has received more attention than his magical ability to create thunder and lightning. He is said to be visible heavenward at times; a vast pair of wings of light spanning a stormy sky. The only other time it is possible to catch sight of the evil *impundulu* is just as he experiences a sexual orgasm when, briefly, he becomes paralysed by ecstasy. It would be possible to kill him at that moment but the few people who have seen him were apparently too dazzled by his feathers to act sensibly.

One white South African who claimed he had seen the primordial *impundulu* wrote: 'And suddenly the landscape was lit up by brilliant sheet lightning. We ran outside the hut and there in the west was a huge dark cloud, almost black, like the breast and head of a bird facing us.'

This observer's African companion pointed to the sky, saying he could see the *impundulu*.

> And then it happened. From either side of the dark cloud – as if the bird grew wings of light – there issued, half round the world it seemed, two bright sheets of lightning like wings enclosing our world.
>
> Every donga showed up. Distant hills and mountains were photographed by eyes. The night, the cloud, the power, and the wing-like illumination gave the Ciskei a beauty of landscape as if an eternal artist had flashed a light on a divine perspective of the earth.

Another divine perspective is presented to Africa by the *momlambo*, queen of love and desire. Her perfect body is shiny and sweet-smelling, as if rubbed with all the perfumes of Arabia. When she walks, the *momlambo* sways and quivers in such a way that men long to ravish her. She lures them on with a certain gesture of her head and a slant of her eyes, which makes men believe she will fulfil their dreams. She is said to possess the charms of all women, magically combined in one goddess.

The *momlambo* enters a man's life like a cool summer breeze over parched veld. Silently, walking on air, she suddenly appears beside him as he walks alone. 'But she has a way of knowing when a man walks alone with ardent desires for a woman filling his mind,' Xhosa storyteller Dwali Nekompela told author B J Laubscher. 'His head becomes like a bucket of water on a woman's head. If she puts no leaves on top, the water spills over the edges. So man's thoughts of beautiful women also spill over – if not during the day, then when he sleeps.'

All men whose thoughts are filled with longing for a beautiful body to caress are known to the *momlambo*. If she fancies a man with such thoughts, she will step out of the unseen into his world – the most beautiful woman he has ever imagined. Nekompela says:

> Sometimes a man with such desires in his heart is walking alone, with only birds and grazing cattle beside him. In the stillness where there was previously no breeze at all a whirlwind suddenly gathers close to him, sucking up leaves and dust from the ground and spiralling along beside him like a moving figure. Then out of the whirlwind comes the sound of gentle, gurgling laughter, until it stops, abruptly. The leaves and the dust drift back to the earth and there, instead of the whirlwind, stands *momlambo*.

Around her head are rows of coloured beads; on her arms

and ankles shiny brass bangles and anklets; on her perfect naked body only a white beaded *inciyo*, her emblem of modesty. He kisses her neck, her glistening shoulders. Then the gurgling laughter stops. His arms are empty. He cannot believe or bear the loss. His heart feels as if it will ache for ever.

He sits in a shady place – miserable and full of yearning, according to the legend – when he hears her lilting laughter, far away at first but drawing nearer. She is suddenly in his arms again, her voluptuous form pressed against him. He begs her to stay, says he wants a second wife, promises he will take more wives to work for her.

She puts her lips close to his ear, blowing words as if they are notes from a reed pipe, telling him they cannot have sex until he has paid dearly for it.

He is mad with love for her, he insists, and will do anything she wants. Anything.

Then she tells him the dark truth: if he wants her body under the same blanket, he must cause the death of his own father. As a reward, she will be his lover, providing him with wonderful crops, rich herds, everything he desires.

Not long afterwards, the legendary man who is in love with the *momlambo* and his father go on horseback to visit some faraway kraals. On their way home, the father's horse stumbles and its rider falls off, breaking his neck. The son becomes wealthy and has many wives, all of whom complain that he is *umtombo otshileyo* – the fountain that has dried up.

While the myth of the *momlambo* might be no more than a sexual fantasy conjured in the imaginations of early Xhosas, why does she make the death of the patriarch the reward for her love? ponders psychiatrist B J Laubscher in *Where Mystery Dwells*. Could her agenda be buried in some other spiritual age? he wonders. Perhaps she comes from that noble line of mythological descent – the classical goddesses of love? Perhaps she is the great supreme female who exercised power over men promiscuously until deposed by the patriarchal cult? Perhaps, to have her love, man must thereafter renounce male rule by killing the patriarch?

* * *

Among the artefacts of witchcraft on display in glass cases at the Lusaka Museum in Zambia are some decidedly bizarre exhibits arranged in three categories: offensive, defensive, and divination.

The offensive items – for settling scores such as jealousy of another's wealth, or revenge for emotional pain caused by adultery – include the *ikulo*, a piece of monitor lizard skin and *chitenge* cloth infused with magical liquid, to be rubbed on the victim's feet when he walks through the offending neighbour's field in order that the neighbour's crops will be transferred to his own field. The *kaliloze* 'gun' is a bit of human leg bone and some beads wrapped in an old rag which, when pointed at another, will cause his death sooner rather than later. The *mukalo wa mumbunda* is a macho-style python skin belt worn by a man who is intending to creep into another's hut to sleep with his wife undetected.

The defensive exhibits, which are charms worn on the body or kept in the hut to combat witches' spells, include the *kilundwe* – bits of genet and python skin and black beads to prevent a corpse being removed by witches. A *kapuyi* comprises bushbaby skin, coloured beads, a tiny carved human figurine and a gourd, which together form magic that permits the owner to have sex with other men's wives with impunity. The *kamandili* is a black gourd with beads to protect the owner from unspecified attack.

One of the viewers at the witchcraft exhibition in Lusaka, a white man who has lived in Africa for many years, told journalist Toni Tilley a story to authenticate a magical charm similar to those on display.

> I was fencing a large farm in Bulawayo, Zimbabwe. While moving some stones, one of the labourers dislodged a black scorpion and was bitten by it. I wanted to take him to the hospital because he needed urgent attention but he refused to go, telling me he had his own medicine for the sting at home in his kraal.
>
> We sent one of the other workers to fetch the remedy: a scrap of rag wrapped around a dried-up baboon finger with filthy claws.
>
> 'You'll get blood poisoning from this,' I told him. He replied that he had been given the medicine by a healer as a cure for all bites and stings, and assured me he had used it successfully before.
>
> By now his hand was very swollen and pus was oozing from the puncture site. I watched with much misgiving as he scratched viciously at the injured hand, drawing a lot of blood. The swelling began to subside almost immediately as pus dripped from the wound. About ten hours later, I looked at his hand and to my amazement could see no trace of the bite or the violent treatment he had administered. Only a few scratches remained.

Among the divination tools on exhibit at the Lusaka Museum are those used by traditional healers to detect the cause of misfortune and to identify the culprit. They include *ngombo ya ku shekula*, a divining basket full of bits of bone and broken mirror, animal skin, shells and figurines; and a hollow antelope horn studded with beads and filled with divination charms.

A number of magical creatures are also on display. 'The *lilombamema* . . . two feet long with the skeletal head of a cougar, the tail of a monitor lizard and a body of rags, beads and snake skins, stared evilly at us from its glass case,' wrote

Financial Times journalist Paddy Linehan from Lusaka.

Informed by a Zambian wood-carver called Aron that a *lilombamema* lived in his village, Linehan wrote:

‘I asked him to explain and he told me this: if a man is having a bad streak he visits his sorcerer who will mix a potion to which the client's own blood is added. There are just a few drops but that is more, Aron pointed out, than goes into one's own offspring.

The client must then rub himself all over every day with the potion, being careful not to lose a drop. In time the liquid becomes rank and tiny life forms appear. They grow and eat each other. The fittest survives and develops into a maggot and then mutates through other life forms until it is a little *lilombamema*. Its appetite grows and so does the luck of its owner.

By now, Aron says, people will become suspicious. The baby *lilombamema* has a mighty appetite and must be fed. First eggs, but later it must have blood – human blood. And it must be blood from the family of its owner.

This means the *lilombamema*'s owner is forced to kill his own relatives, beginning with children. I asked Aron why people didn't do something with the *lilombamema*'s owner since his good fortune and depleting lineage must surely finger him as the "culprit". But Aron declined to comment.

I asked if I could go to his village; if I could stay overnight and see the *lilombamema* for myself. He shook his head slowly and stared. Was I mad? But the next day I asked again and again until he conceded.

On the evening I arrived, everyone was busy: hewing wood, washing clothes, cooking, banging the bottoms of tin containers, putting hens into cages for the night. But the whites of their darting eyes told me they had been warned I was coming. "Whatever you do, say nothing. Pretend you notice nothing."

Aron and I were allocated the circular mud hut. I slept – nay, rested – on the iron bed. Aron snored gently on the earth floor. I must have dropped off because he shook me. And I saw it. It moved slowly in the gloom. It had spikes, I think. A spiny ant-eater?

I looked at Aron. He was as grey as the dawn. He was seeing no spiny ant-eater. I looked again – and it had grown. Its tail was heavier than an ant-eater. It dragged on the ground. Like a monitor lizard's tail. And it flicked.

Oh my, it was evil. It sniffed its way between a few other huts, stopped and looked in our direction. We were perched on a mud heap about 30 yards away. I felt the cold sweat of fear. It licked its lips, I think. It might have had a forked tongue.

We didn't go back to bed. Day came in a rush and people moved around silently rubbing themselves.

On the way back to town, Aron told me they would kill it soon. It wouldn't be too difficult as it wasn't that big yet. It was the first one he had seen but from what he heard they were usually much bigger than this one.

Usually?

Oh yes, they were very common. Every village has them, at least in Zambia.

I asked him what they would do with the body. Nothing, he said. When they were dead they were different; their bodies were made of rags, beads and snakeskins, the clothing of the victims who had nourished it.'

* * *

The Lion Men of Tanzania lurk in the nightmare section of the human mind. But unlike many of the magical figures in African mythology, these sad villains do exist. A cruel testament to the perils of witchcraft belief, they are the sacrificial children of witches, given by their possessed mothers to live among lions in the veld.

Because lions are believed in parts of Tanzania to be ancestor spirits in disguise, the children of people accused of witchcraft are tested in this way to determine if they have inherited supernatural powers. Some are eaten alive, but others who miraculously survive are expected to remain in the bush living as lions themselves.

Alistair Scobie, a journalist who studied ritual murder in Africa during the Seventies, interviewed a young Tanzanian victim of lycanthropy – the magical transformation of human into animal. Once a prevalent belief in Europe in the form of werewolves and vampires, lycanthropy persists in some rural regions of Tanzania despite pleas by the country's former president, the late Julius Nyerere, to eradicate 'all these murders'.

Scobie describes a teenager named Korrogya in the village Mwadui, situated near thornbush terrain favoured by lions. 'He had an open and rather fine face. He spoke good Kiswahili and a lot of English,' says Scobie.

'They broke my legs,' Korrogya told the journalist.

Scobie explains:

> They had not broken his legs . . . Some other cases of this sort had the wrists and ankles broken . . . then tied back in an effort to make them into animal feet. What they had done to Korrogya was to cut the tendons behind his knees, and a horrible mass of scar keloid showed how the operation had been performed.

Korrogya continued:

> My mother gave me, because she was a witch.
>
> To become a witch, a woman gives a child to the lions. Sometimes the child is eaten, sometimes it is not. She must watch to see. If the lions kill and eat the child, then she is a witch. If they do not, then the child may become a lion.

Describing a pit in which he lived with a number of women and children, Korrogya explained:

> . . . They did not do this to my legs until I was ten, I think. I remember very little . . . But I could not walk. I was a lion. We spoke very little. They fed us well, and gave us honey to drink, and much meat. Then they did this thing to my legs . . . We killed several times. We wore the claws.

The claws used by the Lion Men are made of steel, attached to a suit knitted in string fibre. Sewn on to this body stocking are jackal or hyena skins. The Lion Men, fully believing they are wild animals because they have been told so since early childhood, kill under the influence of hypnosis or drugs. Their controllers are the witches who have lived with them for years and who use the Lion Men to terrorise rural communities for their own purposes.

Lions are revered all over Africa. Central to many sacred ceremonies – though none as bizarre as the Lion Men of Tanzania – they are believed in some countries to be the reincarnation of dead chiefs. Many Africans refuse to kill the king of the beasts, who is universally admired for his

A Luo diviner from Kenya. (©Angela Fisher/Carol Beckwith)

The people of Benin – believing their ancestor spirits must be summoned back to earth annually to rebalance a cosmic order upset by human transgressions – invoke the help of a secret Egungun masking society to advise the living. (©Carol Beckwith/Angela Fisher)

Immediately following the death of a Surma woman in Ethiopia, the corpse is wrapped in hides and carried by relatives to its gravesite. With the face exposed so that a blessing of milk can be poured into the ears, the deceased is buried alongside her essential possessions in the belief that she will continue to need such items as her cooking utensils and blankets. (©Carol Beckwith/Angela Fisher)

Overleaf: The Asantehene, King of the Ashanti people of Ghana, wears so much gold jewellery on ceremonial occasions that his arms have to be supported by attendants when he waves to the crowds. Most precious of all the symbols of wealth and nationhood under the king's patronage is the famous Golden Stool, its awesome influence having ignited two wars with the British. (©Carol Beckwith/Angela Fisher)

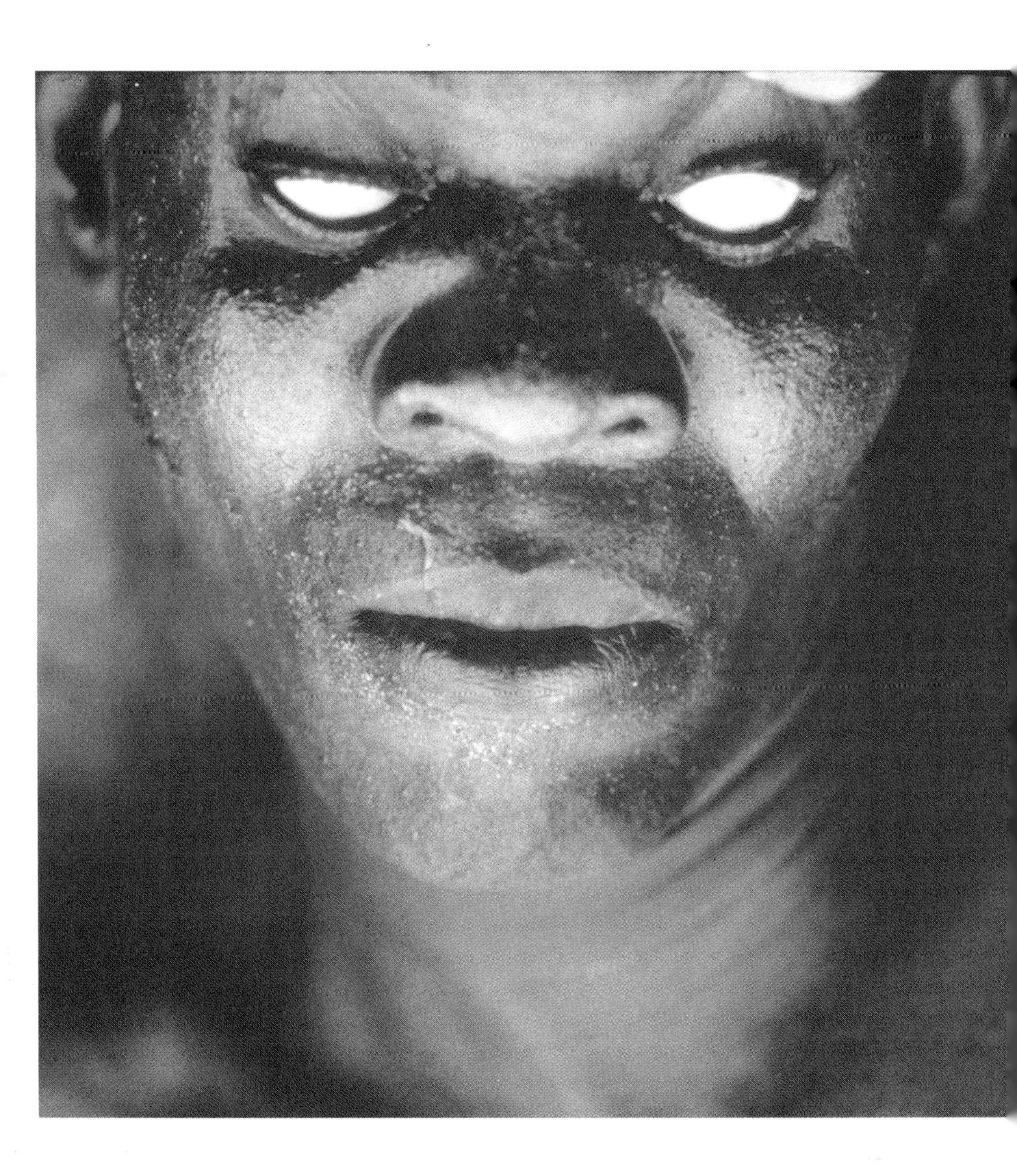

Some African worshippers dance themselves into states of trance so intense that they are believed capable of superhuman feats of strength and endurance. (©Carol Beckwith/Angela Fisher)

Previous spread: An elderly Ghanaian woman pictured in the remote village of Tendang, where suspected witches are banished for life. 'I am sad because I have had to leave my family,' she says. 'I do not think I will ever see them again. I believe my neighbours accused me because they were jealous. I had a good farm and we were doing well, selling our crops. Now I have nothing.' (©Mike Donkin) grandeur and awesome power.

In some communities where lions are fair game, it is customary to fetch the chief living nearest the place of the lion kill so that he can view his 'brother' on the spot where he died.

The slain lion is then skinned and disembowelled by the chief, who must remove from the lion's stomach a ball formed by the undigested fur of creatures the lion has devoured during its lifetime. In order to give himself 'a great roar', the chief must then swallow the ball of hair.

Says Alistair Scobie:

> No one who has seen these animals in their natural surroundings, regal and unperturbed as they take their rest in the shade of some wide-spreading tree, or with feline grace stalking their prey, can fail to be impressed by their majestic appearance. And those who have heard the great cats' call, resounding like some mighty sylvan organ in solemn diapason through the stillness of the tropic night, know that of all the noises with which the African forest can terrify man, none is more awe-inspiring than the lion's roar.

Ten

Spirits of War

Colonial rule in Africa was achieved mainly through warfare. After responding initially with violence, Africans were subdued for long periods during which their apparent compliance concealed underlying tensions. Many of the subsequent resistance movements that militantly gave expression to African aspirations were driven by religious impulses, and most of them were sustained by African magic.

Zimbabwe was born out of guerrilla warfare, a conflict that rewarded successful propaganda above all other tactics. Among its most potent weapons were the spirit mediums who spoke for the country's ancient gods of war – Nehanda and Chaminuka. This is the story of how they were used and abused.

Previously known as Rhodesia, Zimbabwe was the last of

Britain's colonies to achieve independence. The white government's refusal to extend the franchise to the country's black majority meant a negotiated settlement had become impossible by the early Sixties. In 1965, Rhodesia staged its infamous Unilateral Declaration of Independence, provoking a barrage of international economic sanctions but no resolute action from Britain. As a result, the country's nationalist opposition prepared for the first armed attack on the Rhodesian state since the 1896 rebellion. Fourteen years later, majority rule was finally won.

The success of the guerrilla war relied heavily on nationalist fighters – who entered Rhodesia after military training outside the country – being viewed as legitimate liberators. In a country where many African people believe past and present are mediated by ancestral and territorial spirits, the liberation forces had to establish a dialogue with these supernatural forces in order to win popular support for their cause.

That is why, early in 1971, a group of guerrillas who were impatient for action arrived in north-eastern Zimbabwe from neighbouring Mozambique and hid for several days in the forests of the Zambezi Valley. They were waiting to meet an elderly woman called Kunzaruwa, who was the spirit medium of the revered tribal goddess Nehanda. In an interview published in *The Struggle for Zimbabwe* by David Martin and Phyllis Johnson, the leader of the group, Comrade Mayor Urimbo, recalled:

> When we arrived in the area, we had to start by talking to the masses. We spoke to the old people who said we must consult the mediums. We were taken to Nehanda . . . She never bathed and ate only once or twice a week. Her food had to be ground with a mortar and pestle. She hated all European things. We told her: 'We are the children of Zimbabwe; we want to liberate Zimbabwe.'
>
> She was very . . . interested. She knew (a lot) about war and the regulation of war. She said: 'This forest is very, very difficult

> for you to penetrate', but she gave us directions. She told us what kind of food to eat, which routes to take, what part of the forest we were not allowed to stay in or sleep in, where we were not allowed to fight. She said we were forbidden to go with girls and she taught us how to interpret many signs in the forest which would allow us to live safely and to know when our enemy was near.

Urimbo described Nehanda's medium as 'a small woman, very thin and very old, with white hair and skin that was exceedingly black. She was dressed in a piece of black cloth that was wrapped around her body and she wore bangles, some of them gold, on her wrists, and other ornaments around her neck. Her skin was dry and cracked with age, and dung was regularly rubbed on to protect it from the sun.'

Having secured Nehanda's support, the guerrillas drew immense courage from the knowledge that she was on their side, advising and protecting them. Zimbabwe's peasant masses, once convinced that the guerrillas enjoyed the support of their tribal spirits, endorsed the liberation war wholeheartedly.

However, the hideouts in the Zambezi Valley where the guerrillas met for inspiration and information from Nehanda began to be uncovered by Rhodesian security forces in 1972. Fearing Nehanda's frail medium might be captured or killed, the guerrillas decided to take her out of the country. She was initially outraged at the idea and refused to go, but they pleaded with her and she finally agreed to seek safety. They carried the old woman on a stretcher to the banks of the Zambezi, where the powerful magic associated with the river meant the guerrillas had to spend a long time clapping their hands before the medium felt she had been given permission by the spirit to cross into Mozambique. After resting for two weeks in Tete province, they went on to a guerrilla camp at Chifombo on the Zambian border, which was to be Nehanda's new base.

From there, she helped direct the fighters into Zimbabwe for eight months until June 1973, when she died unexpectedly. It was several days before the guerrillas discovered her body because she often went into seclusion without eating for long periods. Her spirit sent word that she should be buried in Zimbabwe, but the war was by then too dangerous for such a move.

Instead, the guerrillas found a temporary burial site along a road they invariably travelled on their journey to Zimbabwe. Nehanda was draped in white and carried to her shallow grave, the bottom of which was softened with leaves. Her body was covered with earth so that she looked as if she were asleep with a blanket pulled up to her chin, with only her head exposed beneath the thatched hut the guerrillas had built over her grave.

The liberation army continued to be guided by the mediums of other territorial spirits throughout the war. When it was over, Urimbo, as national political commissar, praised Nehanda in particular as the leading inspiration in the fighting. 'Her house is still there,' he told journalist David Martin of *The Observer*, London. 'Fire comes and goes but it will never burn. When we crossed into Zimbabwe, we put our weapons there and praised the ancestors and said, "We are going to liberate Zimbabwe." '

Over the years, Nehanda's reputation as protector of soldiers has been celebrated throughout Zimbabwe in music and folklore. One of her mediums, a woman called Charwe, was a major leader of the country's first war of independence in 1896. When that uprising collapsed, she was among the last of the leadership to be captured. Sentenced to death by hanging, Nehanda's last heroic moments secured her a sacred place in Zimbabwe's war mythology. She refused with her final breath to become a Christian, prophesying that 'my bones will rise' in the struggle against the oppressor.

Of equal status to Nehanda among the nation's spirits of war is Chaminuka, a royal ancestor from central Zimbabwe who is said to be Nehanda's brother. Two of the earliest operational zones during the guerrilla war of the Seventies were named after these tribal spirits. Together, they are viewed by many as the founders of Zimbabwe.

Their towering influence over Zimbabwe's masses was not lost on the Rhodesian security forces, who tried hard to counter the advantage scored by the guerrillas in winning the support of Nehanda and Chaminuka during the early stages of the war. Tape recordings purporting to be the voices of mediums denouncing guerrillas were broadcast from helicopters, among many other attempts to reverse the situation. One leaflet, headed TO ALL THE PEOPLE OF THE LAND, was dropped from the air over villages in crucial infiltration areas. It read:

> Some of you have been helping terrorists who came to cause disturbances to you and your families. Your spirits have told your spiritual mediums that they are disappointed because of your action. Mhondoro, your tribal spirit, has sent a message to say that your ancestral spirits are very dissatisfied with you. As a result of this there has been no rain. It is only the government which can help you, but you have to realise your obligation to help the government also.

With both the government and the nationalists promoting traditional beliefs, Zimbabwe's liberation war endorsed ancient spiritual convictions that had begun to lapse among urbanised youth. One guerrilla told David Martin:

> I didn't believe all the things my father used to tell me until I was

> in the bush myself. Then – well, you just had to believe. One time we had no tobacco, nothing to smoke. One of the boys went into a trance. He said that his father's brother had sent us some. His father's brother had died a long time before so we asked him how this would happen. He said that the tobacco would be brought to us by a snake. The body of the snake was all curled up but there in the middle was a lump of tobacco. The boy clapped to the snake very politely and the snake uncoiled itself. Then he took the tobacco and we all had a smoke.

Another sceptic at the start of the war was Josiah Tungamirai, an influential guerrilla leader. 'Personally I didn't believe (in African magic) because I was brought up in the church,' he recalled in an interview with journalist David Martin. But then he met Nehanda at Chifombo in 1972.

> One day the cadres came and told me that Mbuya (grandmother) Nehanda wanted some relish (food). Would (I) fetch a chicken for her. They didn't tell me the colour of the chicken she wanted, so I brought one with white feathers. When I was at the door of her house the chicken collapsed. It didn't die but it just collapsed and stopped making a noise. I asked people about it and they said, 'Sorry, we didn't tell you about the colour. Go and get one with black feathers.' So I did. I went back with it personally and nothing happened. It didn't collapse.
>
> That's when I started thinking about . . . spirit mediums. There must be some science in this. Sometime we must really go deeply into this because there are some wonders (done) by some of these people. When we started the war, these people helped with recruitment. In the villages they are so powerful. If they tell their children they shouldn't go and join us, they won't. When we wanted to go and open a new operational zone we would have to approach the mediums first.

The awesome power of territorial spirits or *mhondoro* comes from their status as the royal ancestors of chiefs of the past, says David Lan in *Guns and Rain: Guerrillas and Spirit Mediums in Zimbabwe*. Believed to be the real owners of the land in Zimbabwe, the spirits of these men are said to protect the fertility of the land and to control rainfall. The most powerful among them – Nehanda and Chaminuka – are said to have lived in the country so long ago that nothing is known of their ancient history.

Support from the *mhondoro* – whether for agricultural purposes or war – is secured through rituals of appeasement, the most important being *kutamba guva* (dance on the grave). Performed within a year of a chief's death, the ancestor is led symbolically out of the bush, where he has been living like an animal, back into his home. From time to time thereafter, beer must be brewed and drunk in the deceased's name lest he feel he has been forgotten – the direst of sins in ancestor worship. *Mhondoro,* which means lion, refers to the belief that a deceased chief's spirit makes its way into the body of a lion while he is living in the bush immediately after death.

Each *mhondoro* controls vast tracts of land. Those who work it must make offerings of grain to their tribal spirit at the first harvest of every season. When outsiders such as sons-in-law settle in a new spirit province, a gift must be given to the *mhondoro* and permission to cultivate the land secured. One young man who changed localities to live with his grandfather explained to author David Lan:

> In the morning my grandfather showed me the field where I could plough. We walked all round the field and then went home. When we reached there we saw a man who was the medium of the mhondoro called Chiwawa. I have never seen this man before. I greeted him but he didn't answer me. I sat down near to him. Then he started to sing and his spirit came out saying: 'Eee. Aaa. Who are you? Get away. I don't want to see you here.' I got up and was about to go but my grandfather said to him, 'This is

your *muzukuru* (grandchild) and my grandchild. He wants to live with his grandfather in this area. Welcome him and look after him well'.

Then the mhondoro said, 'Well, he can stay here but the field you gave him, he mustn't plough it. I will be there checking. Tomorrow I want to give a chicken to this boy.' Then he stood up and went away. I was very surprised. I asked my grandfather, 'What made him do all this?' Grandfather said, 'This is the one who looks after us'. I said, 'Why does he say I mustn't plough my field?' Grandfather said, 'He means you mustn't go to the field early in the morning or you will be eaten by the lions. This is the time that he is working in his land'. I asked, 'Does this mean he has his own lands?' He answered, 'The land of this mhondoro is from Fumhe to Nyarutombo. He is the one who makes the rain fall. If someone breaks his law he can strike him with lightning or make him ill'. I said, 'He wants to give me a chicken. How will he give it to me?' He answered, 'The chicken is not a real chicken. It might be a buck or another wild animal. He means that he will let you catch the buck easily in the forest and that means that you are welcome here'.

Becoming a *mhondoro* medium is a complex process which invariably develops out of a state of physical crisis. The victim becomes ill and neither western nor traditional medicine can cure him. Suspicion begins to grow in the community that the cause of the sickness is spiritual rather than physical. Eventually, a traditional healer recommends that the victim attempts to achieve possession so that the spirit can reveal itself.

Unlike other societies in Africa where possession is spontaneous, in Zimbabwe it happens only in formalised rituals. Beer is brewed, drummers beat relentlessly. The ceremonies, sometimes two or three in a village each week during harvesting, begin shortly after nightfall and might continue throughout the following day. The drums call the spirits, while the father of the stricken individual takes charge of earthly proceedings. The patient sits on a mat in front of the drummers, legs outstretched, head bowed under a white and black cloth. He or she cannot eat, but is free to drink beer.

Female members of the patient's family dance in a half-circle facing the drummers, chanting and singing. Occasionally, a man might leap into the midst of the dancers, cavort dramatically, and then retreat. Experienced mediums come forward to encourage the lurking spirit to appear. They are dressed in black and white, clutching their characteristic axes and spears. As they fall into trance, their dancing becomes more hectic; they act like warriors brandishing weapons, screaming and weeping.

Shortly before dawn, the prospective medium is led into a hut by the presiding party. The mother's relatives wait outside, straining to hear the secrets being revealed while the *mhondoro*'s identity is sought through a question and answer process. The father leads the questioning, along with a traditional healer, both of them knowing that spirits in general are reluctant to speak. They bribe and flatter the *mhondoro*, offering it coins and small gifts that are placed in a wooden plate in front of the aspirant medium. Sometimes the spirit does not speak at all and the ritual has to be repeated another day. Usually, it starts haltingly and then becomes fluent, often delivering long, angry speeches punctuated by moans and anguished sobs.

After being possessed, the patient feels some relief from the symptoms of sickness. Several further possession rituals follow, more information about the spirit is obtained and the patient steadily recovers his health.

The new medium must refrain from sexual intercourse throughout the possession rituals, which might go on for months. The colour red is forbidden in any form anywhere near the proceedings: the *mhondoro* has only to see the colour to die instantly. Every ceremony connected with this ancestral cult takes place on moonlit nights, some only when the moon is full.

Of all the taboos surrounding tribal spirits, blood is the most powerfully prohibitive. Legend claims a *mhondoro* called Chingoo dropped dead when he saw the blood of a guerrilla who had been shot. Apart from the sight of blood on dead or wounded bodies, the merest glimpse of menstruation or childbirth is enough to destroy a *mhondoro*. Tribal spirits must not eat food prepared by a new mother until her baby has cut its first teeth.

The ancestors control life and death. The *mhondoro* invariably wear black and white, symbols of darkness and light, which represent death and life in unity, as opposed to the singular biological life born of woman and symbolised by the colour red.

Black-and-white life belongs to the ancestors. Achieved after death, it is controlled by men, despite some of the most influential *mhondoro* being women. This form of life is considered better than the life created by women out of blood.

Ancestors are wiser than mortals. They cure illness; they know everything about the past and the future; they bring rain and provide protection from witchcraft and bullets. And they live for ever. Their authority knows no bounds; it is a power without end. Although the medium is alive and the spirit is dead, the aura of the *mhondoro* is one of human life being indistinguishable from human death.

Since the *mhondoro* medium is a powerful individual, those who conduct possession rituals must be alert to the possibility of imposters. The aspirant medium is expected to recite the genealogy of the relevant royal ancestor, as well as his history. With only the *mhondoro* supposedly knowing this detail, the medium who recites it convincingly – that is, convincing attending mediums and healers that he has spoken not as himself but only as the vessel of the spirit – is accepted as genuine.

The last test for the aspirant is to select from a collection of carved staffs the one that belonged to the previous medium or the *mhondoro* himself. If he picks the wrong stick, his claim is rejected, although he is not considered fraudulent. It is thought possible that the ancestor simply changed his mind at the eleventh hour, even after the *mhondoro*'s history has been related accurately. No approbrium attaches to the unsuccessful medium once rejected: he must simply find another explanation for his illness.

There are many myths of martyred *mhondoro* – such as Nehanda's bravery during the first Zimbabwean war of independence – but little supporting evidence. An exception is the story of Pasipamire, medium of the prophet Chaminuka, whose life and death were described by Courtney Selous at the end of the nineteenth century.

The English explorer said that he had heard stories from elephant hunters about a very powerful spirit regarded as owner of the land, to whom hunters gave gifts of ivory and cloth in exchange for concessions. Lobengula, King of the Ndebele, sent Pasipamire/Chaminuka 'presents of cattle, young girls, etcetera'. Describing Pasipamire's murder by Ndebele warriors in 1883, Selous said Lobengula had requested that the medium visit his royal seat in Bulawayo. Pasipamire and his wife Bavea set forth at once. At the Shangani River, his small party was attacked by 'the greater part of the (Ndebele) fighting men from the eastern side' of Matabeleland.

> As they advanced Bavea said to her elderly husband, 'They are going to kill you; I know the Matibili. Run! Run! I see blood in their eyes; run! run!' But the old man answered, 'Child, I am too old to run. If this day has come, Chameluga does not fear to die, but bid my son, who is young and swift of foot, creep away in the bushes whilst there is yet time, and carry the news to my people.'

The Ndebele then killed Pasipamire. His son, following his father's instructions, ensured that their village was deserted by the time the warriors arrived to destroy the holy clan.

Embroidered over the years, the myth of Chaminuka claims the Ndebele were unable to kill the prophet with spears. In the end, Pasipamire had to show them how to cause his death – at the hands of a boy who had not yet reached the age of puberty. Before he died, Pasipamire is believed to have predicted and condemned the coming of white colonialists and the death of Lobengula.

Although there is no evidence that Chaminuka participated in the 1896 uprising, the colonialists were aware of the propaganda potential of such a claim and tried to gain intelligence on aspirant mediums who might rally hostility towards the government. In 1903 a woman claiming to be possessed by Chaminuka was observed in a trance by government spies, who reported that she declared: 'I am Chaminuka. I know everything. I am all powerful. I caused the downfall of the Barozwi and the Matabele and I will cause the white man to leave the country. Nothing is impossible to me.' She was immediately arrested, but committed suicide before her trial.

According to extensive research conducted on the subject by historian Terence Ranger in 'The Death of Chaminuka', a few other aspirant mediums tried to claim Chaminuka's power in the intervening years but it wasn't until 1934 that a serious contender stepped forward. Called Muchetera, he had difficulty establishing his credentials because powerful chiefs in his province persistently denounced him as an imposter.

However, Muchetera eventually succeeded in convincing a number of influential white writers and scholars of his authenticity. By the Sixties, when the nationalist upsurge preceding the war of independence got under way, Muchetera took full advantage of the flourishing interest in Zimbabwean culture – especially *mbira* music – to promote himself.

Hence the following overblown account by Michael Gelfand in *Shona Ritual* of Muchetera as he saw his role as Chaminuka:

> At the head of the tribal spirits is Chaminuka and under him are a variable yet large number of tribal spirits . . . who care for large regions of provinces . . . The lesser mhondoro are intended merely to carry messages or news of events to the greater ones, who in turn report to Chaminuka . . . It is believed that all the spirits receive instructions from Chaminuka.

An influential book, *The Soul of Mbira* by P F Berliner, appeared, with Muchetera as its central informant, emphasising the association of *mbira* with Shona religion and with Chaminuka in particular.

> According to (Muchetera), the mbira first came from a place white men had never seen . . . At first the mbira mysteriously sounded from inside a large rock near a circular stone house with no door. People gathered whenever they heard the mbira's music emanating from the rock. The people believed that the voice was that of Chaminuka . . .

Although by then an old man, Muchetera had managed to convince many people, particularly whites, that he/ Chaminuka was the founder not only of Shona politics but

– with his own *mbira* playing recorded on disc and his performance of possession rituals preserved on film – he was also the champion of the nation's religion and culture.

Chaminuka testimonials spun by Muchetera to gullible researchers became embedded in nationalist propaganda. Prominent politician Nathan Shamuyarira declared: 'Mashona reaction looked to the past for comfort and took as tribal hero the tall bearded prophet Chaminuka . . . symbol of . . . resistance . . . a binding factor in resisting the settlers.'

According to Muchetera, Pasipamire's *mbira* players had protected the famous medium from the spears of the attacking Ndebele warriors. They would do so again in the Zimbabwe war, Muchetera claimed. A historian described Muchetera

> . . . prophesying with bravado the inevitable revolution of Zimbabwe's Africans against their European oppressors . . . (the) day 'when European soldiers come to surround my house, firing guns, I will play the ancient songs for the mbira and when the spirit comes to me, I will walk through their bullets without harm.'

But the immortality Muchetera envisaged for himself was not to be. Well established at the zenith of his ambitions, he was suddenly struck down one evening in January 1977, when a group of armed men arrived at his kraal in Makoni district. 'They called at his home and shot him dead,' a witness recalled. 'His *banya* (spirit hut) was blasted. The men ordered that the surrounding people go about their normal duties as usual until after seven days when they were to bury the deceased's bones unceremoniously.'

The killers were neither members of the Rhodesian security forces, nor soldiers loyal to rival nationalist groups. They were the same guerrillas who were waging war in the name of the great prophet Chaminuka. Muchetera lay dead, not because the guerrillas had lost their faith in spirit mediums; on the contrary. The men who shot Muchetera called the people together around his corpse and told them: 'We are fighting a war which is supported by the spirit mediums. We want you to be on our side.'

The reason Muchetera was killed was because he had sought and won white patronage in order to counter the scepticism with which important chiefs viewed his claim to Chaminuka's mediumship. He had adapted the mythology of Pasipamire to flatter the government, giving an entirely different version of the famous prediction. But the words he put into Chaminuka's mouth became his own death warrant.

'Europeans will enter the country and bring peace,' he predicted. 'They will not interfere with your customs and will respect your property. Even poor people will be able to possess cattle without any interference.' It was a version of the famous prophecy which the provincial commissioner of the area found 'uncanny' in its 'accuracy'. His assistant commented, 'Muchetera himself was a really good supporter of the government. He used to (say): "Don't worry. Chaminuka will stand by the government and see that their orders are carried out." '

To the guerrillas, Muchetera's betrayal was unforgivable. Those who killed him were careful to explain why: 'After Muchetera's death they called a meeting . . .' recalled a witness. 'They said that while they were still in Mozambique and trying to infiltrate into the north-east, he went up in a helicopter to drop leaflets against them, saying "I Chaminuka condemn the terrorists." '

The war in Zimbabwe continued without further help or hindrance from Chaminuka. Nehanda's medium was long dead so the guerrillas had to rely on lesser known tribal spirits or traditional healers for the magic most of them believed could win the war.

Healers believed to be selected by the *mhondoro* provided the fighters with various forms of magic medicine which, rubbed into the skin or in some cases swallowed, was said to make bullets turn into water.

Such magic, used in wars all over Africa, was reported by Che Guevara in 1965 to have been 'one of the great weapons in the triumph of the Congolese army'.

Kept secret in Zimbabwe but known as *dawa* in the Congo, it was a liquid made by herbalists from the sap of several magic vines which was poured over the soldiers before they went into battle. A mythical symbol drawn on their foreheads with a piece of coal was said to provide protection against all weapons. Those receiving the *dawa* undertook to abstain from eating, sexual relations and feelings of fear during military action. If they breached any of these taboos, the magic protection evaporated. If anyone was wounded or killed, his comrades assumed he had weakened and eaten food, had sex or felt afraid, thus forfeiting the protection. Few Congolese soldiers would go into combat without *dawa*, a tradition originating in the Stone Age.

Che Guevara wrote in his Congo diary:

> I was always afraid that that superstition would be turned against us and that they would blame us for the failure of some battle in which many men were killed. Several times, I tried to talk with various leaders to convince them not to trust in it. That was impossible; it was recognised as an article of faith. The most politically advanced said it was a natural, material force and that, as dialectical materialists, they recognised the power of dawa, whose secrets were understood (only) by the jungle witch doctors.

Another observer of the powerful belief in African spirits during wars on the continent is Fred Bridgland, journalist and author, who has written extensively about the Angolan conflict:

"The most remarkable thing – and the only truly inexplicable thing – I've seen in my life was in a UNITA base in the forest between Cuban and MPLA bases deep inside eastern Angola in January 1983. I had walked with UNITA for many days to reach Kandende base, commanded by Brigadier Demostenes Chilingutila, who was then UNITA army's chief of staff.

The evening before I was due to leave to head further north into the Angolan interior I was guest of honour, with Chilingutila and my cameraman, at a stunning concert in a floodlit amphitheatre made of wood and thatch, with tiered seats for the troops. The generators which powered the floodlights were Soviet-made and had been captured from the MPLA. There was a modern African ballet; an hilarious spoof on tipsy elders and their wives at a village dance, with soldiers cavorting in drag and others in greatcoats with oversized, laceless boots; a karate display by a team in white bandanas and emerald shorts.

Then the atmosphere began to change. I've never taken drugs, but the music and events that followed I can only compare to being overcome by drugs. There was an unreal, mystic ambience. It began with an amazingly sensuous traditional dance by a wisp of a girl who wowed the soldiers: they whistled and cheered as her navel vibrated and she glided towards Chilingutila. The resident troops sang with a crooner named Mariko: "The people of Angola have been sold as slaves to the Russians, Cubans and the East. When our hope was gone, Savimbi showed us the way. The way was to the bush, to organise and to fight."

Now a lone figure appeared in the arena, clad in greatcoat and boots. He began rolling in the earth while singing a traditional spirit song to the troops, who sang back to music that was haunting, mesmeric. As the singing continued, the floodlights began to fade while in the background a woman kept shimmying into the arena with glowing charcoal on a spade. She piled it up and then got to work with a pair of bellows until it glowed red hot. The performer – still singing back and forth to the troops, still dancing – advanced on the coals and began picking up glowing pieces and placing them on his tongue. He continued to sing and dance – and the troops sang ever more intensely – while placing more and more glowing charcoal on his tongue and moving earlier pieces into his cheek pouches. Eventually his whole mouth was full of glowing embers, shining through his cheeks, and still he was singing and dancing.

It was impossible but the cameraman and I *saw* it, and we've never stopped discussing that evening.

I later asked my Angolan friend Tito, an influential military man, how it was done without damaging the tongue or the delicate lining of the mouth. "African magic," he laughed. What I have no doubt about is, that evening, the UNITA soldiers believed they were summoning the spirits, and the atmosphere was most extraordinary.'

Eleven

The Sacred Stools of Ashanti

Most African uprisings during the colonial era were inspired or sustained by traditional religious symbolism. The Golden Stool of the Ashanti nation in Ghana is the best documented among such symbols.

Representing both ancestral spirits and secular power, the influence of the Golden Stool is so profound that it ignited two wars with the British, who dared to claim it as their own. In a famous gesture of colonial arrogance in 1900, a British governor declared the Golden Stool to be his throne. By custom, not even the Asantehene, king of the Ashantis, is allowed to sit upon it.

Like the Golden Stool, the Ashanti king has religious as well as secular power, being revered as an intermediary with the spirit world and as a national leader. Like most of the kings in Africa, the role of the Ashanti monarch includes priestly functions, since he is the ritual focal point of the kingdom. Bestowed with sacred blessings akin to a god, he is responsible for the prosperity of his people both on earth and in the spirit world. He is worshipped as the terrestrial symbol of the sun; his soul incorporates its radiance. His aura is represented by gold, which is used lavishly to decorate his royal personage during state and religious ceremonies.

When he presides at a ceremony, the Asantehene never walks lest he stumble and disturb the peace of the nation. He arrives in a palanquin shaded by gorgeous, whirling velvet umbrellas, to a fanfare of hundreds of drums and ivory horns. The gold jewellery encrusting his arms is so heavy that bearers have to run alongside his carriage and lift his hands so that he can wave to the crowds. Traditionally, every nugget of gold exceeding a certain weight belonged to the Asantehene, whose goldsmiths have for centuries created jewels and ornaments of international renown as symbols of Ashanti wealth and power. The king often displays a gigantic gold ring on each of his fingers, their emblems representing his many exemplary personality traits.

Following the Asantehene in his long procession on special occasions are teams of soul washers, fan maidens, sword bearers, elephant tail switchers, minstrels, accountants of the royal treasury and guardian warriors. In its midst, if the occasion is important enough, is the most revered spectacle of all: the Golden Stool – 'soul' of the Ashanti nation.

For the first time in a quarter of a century, the Golden Stool was seen in public in 1995 on the anniversary of King Otumfuo Opoku Ware II's succession to the throne twenty-five years earlier. Carried on the shoulders of a royal bearer and shaded by a sumptuous umbrella, its appearance inspired complete silence among 75 000 enthralled guests.

The history of the Golden Stool dates back to 1697, when Chief Osei-Tutu acceded to the Kumasi district of Ghana. At that time, much to Osei-Tutu's dismay, Kumasi was subjected to the rule of the Denkyira nation and paid annual tribute to its king in the form of gold and women. Osei-Tutu was determined to achieve independence and worked for years to form a confederation with neighbouring chiefs. When they were finally united and the Denkyira tribute collectors came to collect taxes, Osei-Tutu mutilated the messengers, filling their coffers with stones. War followed, the Denkyiras were defeated, and their king beheaded.

Osei-Tutu's chief councillor was Okomfo-Anokye, most respected among Ashanti priests. He was celebrated not only as a holy man, but as a great statesman and the architect of the successful Ashanti alliance. Members of this tactical confederation, though jubilant at having dispensed with the oppressor, nevertheless remained autonomous, each represented by an independent 'stool' – the term used for the actual wooden seat, the office of a chief or king, and his immortal soul.

Fearing the hard-won Ashanti union might disintegrate in the months following victory, Anokye set to work on a scheme to provide a common stool in which all Ashantis might exult and unite. Being both an administrator and a spiritual leader, with the conquest of the Denkyira attributed as much to him as to Chief Osei-Tutu, Anokye was in a unique position to create the religious institution he envisaged.

One Friday, after months of careful planning, he summoned all the chiefs of the union to a great gathering at Kumasi. There, in darkness and thunder, amid a cloud of white dust, a golden stool adorned with wonderful ornaments is said to have descended from the sky. It floated to the earth, landing gently on Osei-Tutu's knees. Anokye, hailing the world of the ancestors as well as God the Almighty, declared that the spirit of the entire Ashanti nation now depended on the safety of the Golden Stool.

He then took nail and hair clippings from all the leaders and mixed them with a magic ointment, which he smeared on to the gleaming stool. The remainder of the potion was diluted and sipped by the ruling personages as a sacramental drink, symbolising the fact that the *sunsum*, or soul, of each of them now resided in the Golden Stool.

With this ritual, Ashanti nationhood was sealed around the Golden Stool, which has been protected ever since with the tightest security. It must never come into contact with the earth, and must always lie on its own throne or on a leopard skin, according to anthropologist and Roman Catholic theologian Bishop Peter Sarpong in *Ghana in Retrospect*. It must be 'fed' at regular intervals lest it become hungry, sicken and die, thus destroying all the sacred souls of Ashanti.

The Ashanti nation have gone to extraordinary lengths on several occasions to protect the Golden Stool. In 1896, they favoured it over their king when they submitted to the deportation of Prempeh I rather than resort to a war in which they feared losing the Golden Stool.

By 1897, with virtually the whole of Africa divided up among European colonial powers, Ashanti was a British protectorate. Still burning with resentment that their proud king had been forced to kneel and kiss the feet of the British governor prior to being exiled, the Ashanti hid the Golden Stool and awaited their revenge.

In place of Prempeh came a council of three hated British administrators, and the future under the colonial power looked bleak. But by 1899, the scenario had shifted. The British had begun to suffer setbacks in South Africa and, with trouble brewing in China, the Ashanti calculated that London would be unable to send military reinforcements to the Gold Coast of Ghana in the event of an uprising. Heartened by the turn of international events, they awaited spiritual guidance on how to avenge their king.

At the end of 1899, it was announced in Accra that a new British governor planned to visit Kumasi – capital of the Ashanti kingdom – early in the new year. The Ashantis immediately plotted to kidnap him. They planned to stand aside respectfully while he lectured to them and humiliated their dignitaries and then, when they judged the conditions auspicious, they would seize him and hold him hostage for the return of Prempeh.

London's new man in Ghana was Sir Frederick Hodgson, who was familiar with the Ashanti as he had already spent twelve years on the Gold Coast as colonial secretary. He took the view that 'the natives will respond best to firm handling' and, supremely confident, set forth with his wife – the first white woman to enter Kumasi – to sort out 'the Ashanti problem'.

A great deal of equipment was required both for the journey and for the ceremonies to be conducted by the Governor at Kumasi. Everything had to be transported on the heads of human carriers, with the British officials travelling in hammocks when they grew tired of walking. These crude vehicles consisted of a long pole with a flat two-metre bar at each end, which fitted on to the heads of four men. The canvas hammock, with a shelter for sun and rain, was slung from the pole, and each was dispatched with a spare team of carriers.

There were also teams of personal staff, cooks, cleaners,

orderlies and guards, the whole party numbering at least four hundred. The Governor's personal military escort comprised a mere twenty soldiers as he was not expecting resistance.

Ashanti spies were meanwhile hiding in the dense forests along the route to Kumasi, studying the British approach. At Kwissa, the Governor had arranged to meet the King of Adansi, who sent a supposedly 'insolent' message, although he duly met the British ruler. Afterwards, the Governor remarked to Lady Hodgson: 'Well, I don't like the demeanour of the King and his officials; there seems to be a tendency to truculence and I believe the old man means to give trouble in some way or the other.'

The following day the British party arrived at Kumasi, where they were met by missionaries and a choir of Ashanti schoolchildren singing *God Save the Queen*. Shortly afterwards, an imposing fort – constructed of stone that had been carried by headload from the coast – came into view. It was fifty yards square with circular bastions at the corners and in the centres of the walls, each three yards high and loopholed for musketry. It spoke loudly of the Ashanti armoury, purchased with the nation's abundant gold reserves from Danish traders.

One of the British officers wrote in his diary:

> Nothing astonished me more during my three years in that country than the first sight of this fort, standing out boldly in a wide, open space which, after emerging from the gloomy forest, appeared to me much as the Crystal Palace might to a prisoner released from a dark cell.

The British procession moved up the path leading to the entrance of the fort, amid a fanfare of throbbing drums and twirling umbrellas. On either side sat the assembled

Ashanti chiefs and royalty. As the Governor passed, each rose solemnly from his stool to salute the visitor.

The official meeting took place the following day on the parade ground in front of the fort. The Ashantis formed a semicircle in front of the Governor's chair, their stools arranged in order of seniority, says Frederick Myatt, a British soldier who wrote a book called *The Golden Stool*. At the appointed hour, the Governor strode out of the fort dressed in military uniform and stood to attention to receive a royal salute from a guard of honour. The palaver, as such meetings were known in West Africa, then began.

Sir Frederick Hodgson spoke sternly through an interpreter, warning the assembly that the Ashantis must fulfil the obligations that had been imposed on them by a British treaty twenty-six years earlier. The speech was harsh but its real blow came at the end.

'Where is the Golden Stool?' Hodgson asked. Why had it not been given to him as the representative of the Queen of England? There was no point in keeping it hidden as its power had passed to him, and he wished to sit on it.

Clearly, the Governor did not appreciate the deep spiritual significance of the Golden Stool to the Ashanti people, seeing it merely as a symbol of authority. If he had, he would hardly have made such a provocative demand of an aggressive nation with scant military reinforcements behind him, and he would not have brought his wife along for the confrontation. Whatever his intentions, the stage was now set for war.

During the file past, as the Governor was shaking hands with the Ashanti dignitaries, the Queen Mother of Ejissu touched the Order of St Michael and St George hanging around Hodgson's neck and remarked through an interpreter how much she admired it. Had the Governor known the old woman was one of the main instigators of the planned uprising, he would have run for his life, but he took the remark as a compliment rather than a threat. The Queen Mother was aware that Hodgson had organised an attempt from Accra the year before to find the Golden Stool, guided by a boy who was said to know its hiding place. She also knew the same boy had been smuggled into Kumasi disguised as a member of the Governor's escort, in anticipation of a second attempt to locate the Golden Stool.

After the meeting, the Governor remained at the fort while two of his senior British officers, forty-five Ghanaian constabulary and a retinue of staff went ostensibly in search of arms but actually in pursuit of the Golden Stool. Guided by the frightened boy on the last day of March 1900, they marched to Bali, a village set amid dense groves of plantains, where they established camp for the night.

Early next morning, they began to search the surrounding forest. The quivering boy led them to a group of huts deep among the trees, indicating where the Golden Stool was buried. The soldiers dug for hours, found nothing, and returned to Bali.

There they found the few riflemen who had been left to guard the camp facing a large crowd of armed Ashantis, with many more rustling among the plantains. The British hastily tried to establish a makeshift central post around a few huts but the Ashantis began to close in, their fire increasing.

By now, a starless night sky loomed overhead. The British party crouched inside the windowless huts, their terrified sentries peering through the doorways into darkness. Silence prevailed for some time, and then the drumming began. When it ceased, the Ashantis started to sing. The two British officers, seeing fear mounting on the faces of their riflemen, asked for a translation.

> The Governor came to Kumasi on a peace palaver.
> He demanded money from us
> And sent white men to bring him the Golden Stool.
> Instead of money the Governor shall have
> The white men's heads sent to him in Kumasi.
> The Golden Stool shall be well washed in the blood of the white men.

The war between the Ashantis and the British began in earnest the next day and went on for eight months until December 1900. The Governor was held hostage at the fort in Kumasi for four months, and many lives were lost on both sides.

The British were careful to avoid any covetous reference to the Golden Stool thereafter. But then, to the colonialists' consternation, a scandal erupted unexpectedly in 1920. The sacred Stool was rumoured to have been found by a gang of thieves, who had removed a lot of its gold before hiding the icon underground. The site they chose for its burial was beneath a projected road, where it was found by a party of labourers digging under British supervision. For a time there was tense speculation in colonial quarters as to the likely response of the Ashantis, the Governor going out of his way to assure them that the British had no designs on their Golden Stool. Eventually, the thieves were caught, tried and punished by Ashanti chiefs.

The fort at Kumasi became a regimental museum, for many years attended by an old retired soldier who had been with his father in Kumasi during the siege when the British governor was held hostage. He lived alone in the fort and became an attraction for visitors, to whom he related the long story of the War of the Golden Stool. At night, he claimed, the lonely place was still garrisoned by the ghosts of the old constabulary.

The supernatural character of the famous Golden Stool applies equally to the stools used by Ashanti chiefs. These are carved only from the wood of certain sacred trees, the Ashantis believing humans are not the only beings endowed with immortal souls: lower animals have souls, too, as do some trees and plants.

The traditional Ashanti stool-carver, a religious craftsman of exemplary standing in the community, had to appease the spirit of each tree before he felled it, sacrificing eggs, a fowl or even a sheep in the process. According to Bishop Peter Sarpong, the stool-carver might say: 'Tree, here is a chicken for you. I am going to make a stool out of you; receive this offering and eat. Please, let not the tool cut me. Do not let me suffer afterwards; and let me have a good price for the stool.'

Even today, the stool-carver's tools must have a spiritual rite performed over them before he embarks on an important commission, or when the job in hand is not proceeding satisfactorily. Palm wine is poured over them, or they are sprinkled with the blood of a chicken, while prayers are offered to the ancestors.

The design incorporated in each stool has a special significance, indicating either the social status of the individual who will sit on it or his ancestry. Important stools – or shrines, as they become once a revered owner dies – must rest on stools of their own, the shrines of the gods being displayed on special crocodile stools during public functions.

The ceremony conducted to bestow chieftainship is known as 'enstoolment' among the Akan people of Ghana, including the Ashanti. As soon as the chief is enstooled, he becomes sacred, a status endorsed by numerous taboos including that he may not strike, or be struck; he must walk with great care lest he stumble, and never barefoot; his buttocks should not touch the ground. His foremost function is to perform religious duties, administrative roles being less important. Neglect of holy responsibilities will lead to his 'destoolment'.

Although every Akan person owns at least one stool, only select members of the community are accorded the great honour of having their stools 'blackened' for posterity after their deaths. Chiefs and royalty are the most likely recipients of this rite, but extraordinarily courageous or altruistic commoners might also be immortalised in this way when they die.

A chief possesses many stools but only one of them is blackened, its selection often giving rise to lengthy debate. It may be the one on which he habitually ate his meals; the one on which he sat to take his daily bath; or the one on which his corpse was bathed and embalmed before lying in state prior to burial.

The blackening ceremony is described in detail in Bishop Peter Sarpong's book *The Sacred Stools of the Akan* by a man who served as a stool-carrier, itself a religious role, to the Paramount Chief of Offinso state:

> On a previously appointed day, which is made known well in advance to the sub-chiefs of the state, all the ancient stools are assembled in the open hall of the chief's house.
>
> The new one about to undergo the ceremony is put amongst them. Beginning from the oldest to the newest, the new chief pours libation with palm wine on each stool to invoke the blessings of the good ancestors on such an important function, and on the whole state. Then eggs are broken and, in a calabash or earthenware bowl, mixed with soot collected from the kitchen.

> The new stool is smeared with the mixture until it becomes as black as coal. After this, a sheep is killed and its blood sprinkled on the stools . . . Its fat is carefully collected and put on them. Then prayers are said for the prosperity of the nation, and the stools returned into their temple.

The soot used in this ceremony must be of a particular kind. Around the stove in the chief's house are many spiders – considered especially wise creatures by the Ashanti – which duly spin their webs. Over time, the webs collect soot, and they are then mixed with eggs to anoint the wisdom of dead rulers. The webs – designed to capture insects, making them the prey of the spider – symbolise the dead chief's power both in life and as an ancestor: metaphorically, to cross a chief is to entangle oneself in misfortune.

Eggs are significant because, being delicate objects, they warn the living to treat the stool shrines of their ancestors with great care. As eggs contain no bone or hard material, they are considered peaceful. When an Akan individual thinks he has been defiled and wishes to cleanse himself of evil, he uses eggs in a ceremony to show his soul is now at peace.

Once blackened, the stool is kept with all the other shrines in a windowless temple, or stool-house, within the chief's residence, explains Peter Sarpong in *The Sacred Stools of the Akan*. There the chief keeps watch over all the stools, giving them food when he is himself eating. Official stool-bearers are permitted to go into the temple with the chief, but under no circumstances must whites enter, nor any citizen from an enemy state, nor a person who has recently undergone circumcision. Menstruating women never venture anywhere near the stool-house.

Enstoolment of a chief takes place in a secret ceremony conducted inside the stool-house, the accompanying celebrations outside the temple having no religious significance.

Away from the public eye, he strips naked and, supported by priests, is lowered three times over the stool of the most renowned ancestor. His first act as chief is to arrange the funeral rites of his predecessor. A grand vigil is kept on the eve of the funeral, with the late chief lying in state in the stool-house (although some Akan people deem it improper for a living chief to have any contact whatsoever with death or corpses).

Thus, a chief begins his reign from the stools of his ancestors, works among the ancient stools on a daily basis, reminded of his ancestors each time he takes a mouthful of food, and finally departs this world surrounded by the awesome blackened stools. Their influence dominates every ceremony conducted in Kumasi and neighbouring communities, and every royal occasion. 'Without them, the religion of ancestor worship among the Ashantis would be virtually meaningless,' says Bishop Sarpong.

And without religious symbols like the Golden Stool giving impetus to African resistance wars – such as those waged in Ghana and Zimbabwe – the nationalism which conquered the colonial era would have been slower to develop on the continent.

Tanzania's Maji Maji Revolt in 1905 – another example of the utilisation of traditional religious ideas to achieve national unity – gave rise to the Tanganyika African National Union (TANU), a political party that eventually secured independence in Tanzania. 'It is true that a source of salvation cannot hide itself from the people . . .' wrote historian G C K Gwassa of the spirit of freedom evoked by belief in Maji Maji.

Speaking at the United Nations in 1956, Tanzania's new leader Julius Nyerere noted:

They (the Maji Maji) rose in a great rebellion not through fear of terrorist movement or a superstitious oath, but in response to a natural call, a call of the spirit, ringing in the hearts of all men, and of all times, educated and uneducated, to rebel against foreign domination . . . Its (TANU's) function (was) not to create the spirit of rebellion but to articulate it and show it a new technique.

Twelve

Perspectives on African Religion

The study of African religion is a relatively new field of popular research, still preoccupied with myths, rituals, gods and ceremonies. Little has been written about the moral complexities which lie at the heart of African spiritual beliefs, involving concepts of individuality, destiny and social ethics.

Critical among these beliefs is the African philosophy which strives to balance collective identity with individuality – the realm in which African mores depart most radically from western norms. Although recognising that everyone is uniquely endowed with individual personality, abilities and motivations, in much of Africa the communal interest is emphasised over individual freedom. Each community member is viewed primarily as a constituent of the group: it is the community which defines the individual, rather than his personal characteristics. As the noted African theologian John S Mbiti has succinctly expressed it: 'I am because we are, and since we are, therefore I am'.

Although there is scope for individual achievement and expression, it never extends to the western idea of individualism whereby people view themselves as independent of their social and historical circumstances. Everybody in African traditional society interacts throughout life with communal precedents, destiny, natural and supernatural forces in order best to achieve the harmonious integration of the self with the wider world.

This unifying philosophy, reflected in cultures all over Africa, is well expressed in the southern Sudan by the Dinka concept of *cieng*, meaning 'morality' or 'living together', depending on context. Anthropologist Francis Deng explains in *Africans of Two Worlds*:

> On its highest level of abstraction, cieng is a guiding force above Dinka community process. It aims at an ideal social order in which people are united in full harmony, with no quarrels or frictions and with mutual indulgences. On the lowest level, it requires and generally achieves conformity with the sum total of community expectations, which are in fact segments of the ideal.

The purpose of *cieng* is contentment, which the Dinka associate with *wei*, meaning life or soul. 'Harmony is best achieved by attuning men's demands and desires to the mythical (gods and ancestors), living superiors, and other fellow men,' says Deng.

The Dogon people of Mali consider that, because all human actions and circumstances are inextricably connected to the functioning of both the natural and the supernatural worlds, humans have many souls rather than just one soul forming the essence of a person, as most westerners believe.

Unlike many philosophers in the west, the Dogon do not see humans as essentially unchanging beings but as dynamically developing clusters of forces whose powers increase or diminish in accordance with individual moral and spiritual actions. They believe new-born infants are only potentially human and must await social and spiritual identity, bestowed by the community as the child grows to puberty.

The Yoruba of Nigeria focus on the relationship between destiny and personality. Like the Dogon, they believe humans have multiple souls. More important, however, is their concept of the *ori*, meaning 'head', which has two dimensions: one resides inside the individual and constitutes the personality or ego, while the other is located in heaven and is the alter ego or guardian soul. The *ori* is, in effect, the incarnation of an ancestor.

The Yoruba believe the ancestor *ori* in heaven chooses a person's destiny – character, talents, success – before he is born. To nurture this destiny effectively, the *ori* must receive assiduous ritual attention on earth. The *ori* is respected above the gods: what he refuses, the gods cannot grant. Unfortunately, the *ori* can be careless and make mistakes, in which case the individual ends up with a bad destiny and only his *ori* to blame for it. Because witches and angry ancestors can spoil a good destiny, everyone must be aligned with a powerful divinity – usually a god common to all members of a particular lineage – to act as protector. According to the Yoruba, life is on the one hand preordained yet on the other capable of modification by personal and spiritual behaviour, an individual's character, as well as his *ori*.

The Tallensi of Ghana have a slightly different understanding of personal destiny, explains anthropologist Benjamin C Ray in *African Religions: Symbols, Ritual and Community*. Like the Yoruba and Dogon, they believe an individual's inner life is directly linked to his social history in all its individuality and uniqueness. The Tallensi also believe their individual destiny – which does not emerge fully until puberty and is the deciding factor in a person's success in life – is prenatal and selected in heaven. During childhood, this destiny – like social identity – is closely linked to the mother. A sick child is believed to be suffering from a sin of its mother's destiny rather than its own.

Only when the Tallensi child reaches adolescence does it assume its own destiny. At puberty, a youth is guided by society, rather than his parents, in the form of ancestor spirits who mediate his maturing prenatal destiny. These ancestors reveal themselves during critical adolescent experiences, such as illness. Once their presence has become known to the Tallensi youth through divination, a destiny shrine is erected for him at which he and his father then make sacrifices to the guardian ancestors who will determine his success or failure in life. Emphasis on the power of the ancestors rather than the arbitrary influence of the prenatal fate marks the shift in life towards maturity and moral responsibility as the youth acquires the right and freedom to exert his own personality. It is his own moral behaviour, guided by his ancestors, which thereafter determines his destiny.

The Tallensi senior son's destiny shrine shifts throughout his life, expressing the phases of his changing social identity. First, it is located in his mother's quarters; then in his wife's, though within the sphere of his father's influence. Until his father's death, the son lives in his father's household subject to the dominant influence of his father's all-powerful destiny. The two use separate entrances to the family compound so as to avoid meeting each other unexpectedly in a symbolic clash of destinies. When the father dies, the eldest son relocates his shrine to the main entrance of the household alongside the clan's ancestor shrines, which guard the whole settlement.

Traditional Tallensi women never transcend the influence of their prenatal destiny to acquire independent social status. Theirs remains an arbitrary fate throughout life, most dramatically revealed in the illness or death of children. Sometimes, when a woman suffers too many reversals of fortune, an exorcism of the prenatal destiny may be performed. The same remedy is offered to men who habitually fail to become morally responsible adults. Through ritual ceremonies, the prenatal destiny is transferred to an animal or some other object and thrown far away from the compound into a barren place. If this fails and the prenatal destiny continues to dominate, society rationalises that the individual is a victim of his or her fate and evermore will be doomed by it. Very often, these luckless victims are socially marginalised people whose failure to become mature adults is due to mental illness. Since prenatal destiny is essentially an amoral concept, confirmation via divination and ritual that an individual is unable to assume moral responsibility releases both the individual and the family from the guilt of repeated failures in life.

People achieve personal freedom in the Tallensi view only if they achieve moral responsibility, a notion that has been compared by some anthropologists to the idea of the subconscious. Destiny is seen as a hidden element of the self, sometimes controllable, depending on the individual's willingness to conquer amoral desires and conflicts imposed by the subconscious. Success in this battle determines success in life.

These are some of the variables in African religion regarding the soul and the relationship between individual and community.

Another fundamental feature of traditional religion in Africa is the relationship between the living and the dead, which exerts a powerful psychological influence over most societies on the continent. Not overly concerned with ideas about an afterlife in the sense of a new existence in heaven, most Africans believe it is the way in which the dead continue their involvement in this life on earth that matters. Human life does not end in some sort of transcendent future: the important time for the dead is the present and the important place is on earth among the descendants. Immortality exists as a practical reality in the daily life of the living community.

There are, however, a number of exceptions in which the notion of an afterlife is central to death rituals in Africa. The Dogon of Mali conduct elaborate ceremonies to usher the dead out of the world of the living and into a region called Manga, meaning paradise. The deceased travels for about three years through blistering heat on a punishing journey of retribution for misdeeds committed on earth. Once the purgation is completed and the soul redeemed, it proceeds to paradise, where it remains for ever in an idealised state, sitting under a canopy of trees in the perpetual cool of evening.

In Nigeria, the Yoruba believe 'all we do on earth, we shall account for kneeling in heaven'. The *ori*, or ancestor soul, goes to heaven to receive judgement before God. If the person seeking redemption makes the grade, he goes to the 'good heaven', which is free of suffering. Once there, the deceased can choose a new destiny and return to earth as a child: it is said that the same *ori* may be reborn in several children simultaneously. At the other end of the moral spectrum is the 'bad heaven', an unbearably hot and arid place.

Deceased LoDagaa people from northern Ghana undergo an elaborate process of judgement and redemption culminating in a series of ceremonies known as the Cool Funeral Beer. Until these rituals begin, the soul is believed to have been suspended above the tree tops since death, unable to go into its former hut but also unable to proceed to the realm of the ancestors. A shrine is carved from a branch of a special tree, which is believed to fall into the lap of the deceased's eldest son. Said to be the 'father', this branch sculpture is a material symbol of the soul of the deceased falling into his son's realm, as well as an altar through which to communicate with the deceased. Its existence – the symbolic substitution of the dead person by a concrete representation – marks the moment of transformation into the world of the ancestor spirits.

During this ceremony, the LoDagaa deceased embarks on his final journey, travelling west towards the setting sun, to a place known as the Country of the Great God. The first hurdle is the River of Death, where the dead soul pays a ferryman with money left in the coffin by relatives. If the deceased has not led a good life, he will fall through the bottom of the ferry and must swim across the river, a mission which takes three years. If the deceased owed money or anything else when he died, he must wait on the opposite bank until those to whom he is indebted arrive and are repaid. If the dead soul has been a witch, she must eat her own arm and leg before crossing another river without a ferry.

Once in the Land of the Dead, the deceased is put through a number of ordeals, their severity and duration being determined by the magnitude of past sins. When he arrives, the dead person must sit on the top of a tree under the hottest of suns. If he had a good heart, he might sit there for three months; if he had an evil disposition, for six months; if he was a witch, for three years; if a rich man, for three years. The heavy penalty for wealth reflects the widespread traditional African belief that many others suffer in order for a few to accumulate riches.

Final judgement is based on the notion of collective rather than individual redemption: the moral worth of one is not evaluated beyond the worthiness of his clan. It involves everyone being divided into kinship groups. If any of these contain an undue number of witches, liars, thieves or cheats, they will receive only misfortune, with only salt water to drink, in the Land of the Dead. The good groups, meanwhile, receive all the pleasures they enjoyed in life. Men in the good groups merely have to imagine what they want in order to get it, whereas those in the bad category have to labour much harder than they ever imagined necessary on earth.

While God does sit in judgement in the death rituals and beliefs of some African societies, he has little responsibility for the moral behaviour of living people. The ancestors are the custodians of moral values on earth. Many African societies are governed for all practical purposes by genealogical systems rather than political states, with ancestors at the heart of their religious and administrative functions. This is not because the dead exert a particularly potent fear in the overall philosophy but because the social code is defined by them as unassailably respected elders with the wisdom to conduct the destiny of the community on earth. They are elevated beyond the transient muddles of life; unequivocally superior beings with sacred power over the morality of ordinary mortals. They are, says Benjamin Ray, 'the ritualization of society's rules'.

The ancestors control social relationships throughout Africa. They are the cement which holds the social order together. As the child owes its parents respect, so the parents owe their ancestors obedience and reverence. The ancestor spirits retain a parental role at the religious, supernatural level of community affairs.

Benjamin Ray relates a good example of the influence exerted by ancestors on kinship relations which have gone awry. Pu-eng-yii, a Tallensi man who left his own family to join another kinship group in pursuit of financial success, was severely injured in a car accident. In consultation with a diviner, he was told that his ancestors had caused the accident in retaliation for his rejection of his own family: if he did not make urgent ritual reparation to his ancestors, they would eventually kill him. Pu-eng-yii followed the diviner's instructions, apologising to the ancestors and demonstrating his remorse through various sacrifices. He then returned to his own clan.

Although the ancestors are believed to inflict punishments such as illness and even death, the suffering they bring is purely an inducement to good behaviour and is always seen as a necessary societal regulator, not as evil. Wickedness is another issue entirely.

Benjamin Ray explains:

> Unlike Western religions, African thought does not conceive the source of evil to be a fallen god or spirit like Satan or the Devil. Instead, the source of evil is located in the human world among the ambitions and jealousies of men (and women). The source of evil is thus demonic humanity: the witch or sorcerer.
>
> The image of the witch . . . is the image of an inverted or reversed human being. Witches . . . act only at night, fly or walk on their hands or heads, dance naked, feast on corpses . . . murder their relatives, live in the bush with wild, even predatory, animals . . .
>
> This symbolic image is consistent with the sociological image of the witch . . . as an antisocial person: morose, unsociable, disagreeable, arrogant, ambitious, sly, ugly, dirty, lying, envious, shifty-eyed, staring. The witch . . . is thus an antisocial person and an anti-human being.

But the power of the witch comes from the sacred realm of African understanding – the supernatural – just as surely as the power of priests, chiefs and prophets does. The inversion exhibited by the witch, a sign of sacred power, is sometimes also seen in the diviner and derives from an equally sacred source: they differ only in that one uses the power to destroy and the other to create.

The Lugbara people of Uganda believe witches have the inverted characteristics of ancestors and prophets, inversion being seen as a sacred sign to be used either for good or ill. In the Lugbara view, good lies in stability and social harmony while all radical forces are by definition *onzi*, meaning any power which changes divine relations. The world of the witch is a complete reversal of the sacred order, and is therefore *onzi*, a word which loosely translates as evil. 'A witch is a chief,' claims a Shona proverb often quoted in Zimbabwe by mourners who believe witchcraft lies behind their bereavement: it implies that witches are above the law, like despotic chiefs. What distinguishes the witch from the diviner or wayward chief is not evil, but perverse motives. A prophet is inspired by divine inspiration to help the community: witches are motivated by envy or greed to cause misfortune.

The witch is an outcast because she represents those urges and instincts which, left unchecked, would destroy society. That is why witches are associated with deformed beings who by definition are not fully integrated members of society.

Anthropologist Mary Douglas has observed of the Sudanese Dinka that their witchcraft concepts are an assessment of human nature in general. 'For them,' she writes in *Implicit Meanings: Essays in Anthropology*, 'hell is other people.' It is the 'unique individual', the unconditional egotist, whose behaviour subverts the social order. In a kinship-based society, evil is self-willed individualism exploiting society for personal gain. This image, so pervasive in the west, is emphasised by Douglas' observation that 'the witch is demonic precisely because he is so resolutely finite, banal, self-determined' in a world governed by sacred powers.

Another widespread religious concept in Africa is the rite of passage in a multitude of forms and ceremonies, which gives sacred meaning to human events. Its significance is conferred in three ritual sequences of separation, transition and reincorporation, their objective being to create meaningful transformations in the life cycle – from birth to puberty to marriage to death. Rites of passage apply also in the ecological sphere and the temporal cycle – from planting to harvest; from seasonal changes to New Year.

According to Benjamin Ray:

> The important phase in these rites is the middle or liminal phase of transition. In this phase people are metaphysically and sociologically remade into 'new' beings with new social roles. Newborn infants are made into human persons, children are made into adults, men and women are made into husband and wife, deceased people are made into revered ancestors, princes are made into kings. Seasonal transitions are also marked and celebrated in this way: thus the old year is made into the new, and the season of drought is made into the season of rain.

This re-creation of people and time is the symbolic destruction of the old and birth of the new. During the ritual liminality, people and time are both destroyed and renewed; they are neither what they were nor what they will be. The time between seasons and years belongs neither to the old nor the new. 'It is a time out of time,' explains Benjamin Ray, 'when the usual order of things is reversed and thrown back to primordial chaos . . .'

The traditional northern Ashanti of Ghana, for example, celebrate their New Year through a ritual involving the reversal of normal behaviour in order to bring about moral refortification. Called the Apo, meaning to speak harshly, it is a brief period between years when hostilities are openly aired, especially against the King. Harbouring grudges is believed by the Ashanti to harm both parties in a dispute. During the Apo, people release the dangerous feelings which can lead to witchcraft in order to proceed afresh.

Says an Ashanti priest:

> Our forebears . . . ordained a time, once every year, when every man and woman, free man and slave, should have the freedom to speak out just what was in their head, to tell their neighbours just what they thought of them . . . When a man has spoken freely thus, he will feel his sunsum (soul) cooled and quieted, and the sunsum of the other person against whom he has now openly spoken will be quieted also. The King of the Ashanti may have killed your children, and you hate him. This has made him ill, and you ill, too: when you are allowed to say before his face what you think, you both benefit.

The Apo involves the normal rules and structure of society being suspended: people of high rank are brought down to the level of commoners to be humbled and chastised by ordinary mortals. Regardless of whether this ritualisation of criticism actually relieves social tension, it expresses the moral idea that grudges, especially towards people in authority, should be put aside for the future benefit of society as a whole.

During the Apo, a festive atmosphere prevails in the streets, with even the gods emerging from their sanctuaries to meet and greet. Their shrines are then washed and purified in river water, symbolising that even they have become polluted during the past year. On the first day of the New Year, the King performs an animal sacrifice marking a return to the normal social order for the next twelve months, until the cycle of the year comes around again, when symbols of order are once more reversed to keep power in perspective.

* * *

The way people view the world around them reveals how they evaluate life. From earliest childhood, the Igbo of south-east Nigeria trust their cosmology, which explains how everything came into being and informs their entire belief system. Through it, they know how to behave towards their gods and ancestral spirits, as well as their fellows on earth.

Although trust in their cosmology is a feature of most societies on the continent, few Africans speculate about the origins of the universe. Benjamin Ray explains:

> African thought tends to be bound up with daily life and hence there is little interest in questions that do not concern practical matters. Most African myths deal primarily with the origin of man and with the origin of certain social and ritual institutions that account for real-life situations. These myths explain the basic conditions of human life as the people now find it.

The world through Igbo eyes is a good and peaceful place populated by all the beings and things in creation; heavenly and earthly, animate and inanimate. The spirit world is the realm of the creator, the gods and the ancestors – as well as the future abode of the living after death. Igbo existence, like that of many other Africans, is a dual interaction between the visible and the invisible, the spiritual and the material, good and bad, living and dead.

The dead are very much part of Igbo society. A lot of activity goes on among dead people, who retain their personalities, laughter and thoughts, as well as continuing the lineage system just as they did on earth. Natural death in very old age is a matter for joy rather than sorrow because it is an index of high status among the ancestors: the older one dies, the better, because seniority determines rank, alongside royal status, among the ancestors.

Although the world is seen through Igbo eyes as a benign place, its balance is continually under threat from natural and social disasters. Events such as drought, floods, lightning strikes and disease epidemics, as well as antisocial human behaviour and violation of taboos, are ever-present to challenge the equilibrium of the world. The Igbo believe these disturbing forces can be controlled, however. By manipulating the causes of misfortune through divination and magic in various ritual forms, and by appealing for the intervention of the ancestors against malignant powers, they attempt to maintain social and cosmological balance, explains anthropologist Victor Uchendu in *The Igbo of South East Nigeria.*

The untimely death of a young person is among the greatest challenges to the concept of cosmological balance. Such a death creates widespread uncertainty which must be allayed by identifying the cause of death through divination. The diviner may attribute untimely death to sins committed by the deceased during a previous life, or perhaps to a breach of sacred taboo often ascribed to acts of witchcraft that may have occurred without the knowledge of the innocent deceased. By following prescribed ritual purification ceremonies designed to dissociate the living from the deceased's sins, cosmological balance is restored.

The maintenance of balance in the universe is a constant preoccupation among the Igbo, to the extent that anything which threatens the well-being of the community – such as too much rain or not enough rain – is a warning that the situation needs adjustment before it creates havoc. Because they believe all misfortune can be avoided through sacred intervention, there is constant manipulative recourse to the spirit world.

Reciprocity is the principle most highly rated in Igbo social relations. A relationship that is seen as unbalanced in either obligation or reward is viewed with dismay as a precursor to trouble. This is reflected in Igbo legal processes, where resolution ideally involves compromise. The outright victor in a case is more likely to be met with scorn than applause.

Although individuals, including ancestor spirits, are expected to be motivated by self-interest, this tendency must be tempered by obligation in order to be mutually beneficial. 'It is only proper that the left and right palms should wash each other so that both might be clean', cautions a much-quoted Igbo proverb.

Central to the philosophy of reciprocity is the Igbo realisation of human interdependence, which is summed up in the maxim of 'helping others to get up'. The individual who helps others commands respect, while the selfish ones who 'fail to hear one's cry' are treated with suspicion, often becoming the targets of witchcraft accusations because they are seen as hindering social balance through their independence.

The ideal of interdependence extends to the world of the ancestors. Reciprocity requires that the ancestor spirits be honoured and offered continual sacrifices, often including a portion of food and drink each time the living have a meal. In return, an obligation of protection is imposed on the living dead. Because imbalance among both the living and the dead heralds calamity, it is through mutual dependence and the belief that malevolent forces can be manipulated that the Igbo achieve equilibrium.

Victor Uchendu explains:

> If you ask the Igbo why he believes the world should be manipulated, he will reply, 'The world is a marketplace and is subject to bargain'. In his view, neither the world of man alone nor the world of the spirits is a permanent home. The two worlds together constitute a home. Each world is peopled with 'interested'

individuals and groups and much buying and selling goes on in each. People go to the marketplace for different reasons, but the common motivation is the desire to make a profit. Although the profit motive is the guiding factor, there are occasional losses. From the Igbo point of view, a person does not abandon trading because he suffers losses. It would be cowardly to do so, but he cannot carry on indefinitely if he does not balance his losses with gains.

This idiom is dramatised every time a mother goes to the village market, says Uchendu. As she packs her wares and hoists the basket on to her head, her children come to her individually and chant:

Mother, gain from market people;
Market people, lose to mother.

Each child spits into the mother's cupped hands and she then rubs her palms together, symbolically cleansing her face to achieve 'good face' for the commerce ahead. This daily ritual is based on the principle of social balance in that it involves bargaining to achieve compromise between buyer and seller.

Another vital virtue in Igbo eyes is transparency, especially important in a society where the individual is believed to have scope to manipulate the universe to his own advantage.

Victor Uchendo says:

Igbo are a people who tend to wash their dirty linen in public. Anyone who has overheard Igbo co-wives quarrelling will appreciate this point. The compact household units, the matter-of-fact approach to sex, the symbolic way 'transparency' is conveyed by tasting food or drink meant for the visitor or neighbour, the respect accorded to the leader who has 'strong eyes' to see 'hidden things' and the 'mouth' to expose them are

> indicative of their transparent orientation. The concept of the good life among the Igbo is so built on the transparency theme that the individual dreads any loss of face. The major deterrent to crime is not guilt-feeling but shame-feeling.

Igbo leaders are expected to be accessible to everyone, as well as transparent to an exemplary degree in their dealings. Even friendships which have become strained might resort to *igbandu*, a ritual designed to restore confidence, in which one is required to drink the blood of the other. Host and visitor, patron and client, doctor and patient may seek strengthened relations by ritually swearing fidelity. This reflects the no-nonsense nature of the Igbo, who requires demonstrable reassurance of good faith because he knows that some people might not uphold ideal ethics unless constrained to do so.

An ancient Igbo legend, featuring a local philosopher and a foreign visitor who has made disparaging comments about Igboland, illustrates the importance of transparency:

> 'Do you say that my country is bad? Can the earth or trees or mud walls speak? How do they offend?' demands the philosopher.
>
> 'No,' replies the foreigner, 'they don't.'
>
> 'Well answered,' sneers the philosopher. 'Never speak badly of my country again. Should any of my people offend you, accuse them directly.'

This mythical philosopher's attitude points to the widespread practice of scapegoating that lies at the heart of witchcraft accusations. When misfortune strikes, the people who lack transparency by employing half-truths, deceptions or any lack of candour, are immediately in the firing line because they exhibit antisocial behaviour.

Yet the scope for individual freedom of choice fostered by Igbo culture allows for innovation. Victor Uchendu tells us:

> There is opportunity for experimentation as well as tolerance for failure and admiration for success. The most important factor for the acceptance or rejection of an innovation is its status implications for the individuals and groups concerned. The crucial question is this: Will the acceptance of this innovation 'make the individual or the town get up?'

The world through Igbo eyes may be fraught with censure but is also full of opportunity. 'One who is over-cautious of his life,' says a favourite proverb, 'is always killed by the fall of a dry leaf.' Tackling life's challenges in order to 'get up' may involve aggression, bribery or magic – if one can get away with these devices. What it will certainly involve is perpetual vigilance of one's own ethics as well as those of competitors.

The overriding philosophy of Igbo life is egalitarianism: no individual or group should acquire undue control over the lives of others, and all citizens should have an equal opportunity to achieve success. 'A child who washes his hands clean deserves to eat with his elders,' says a proverb which acknowledges achievement beyond the rigidity of normal social structures.

A talented individual who achieves wealth and 'makes the town get up' might even be permitted to wield some power over his elders. 'No one knows the womb that bears the chief,' is an Igbo warning that chieftainship is not a divine right: once achieved, it must be continually validated.

A leader wins support for as long as 'he does not govern too much', says another proverb. The Igbo grant him minimal power which can be rescinded, and judge him on his egalitarian 'get up' ability. As leadership constraints, these community ideals form an ideological barrier to strong central authority.

Among the many traditional rituals which further Igbo community ideals is the *ofo*, a hand-held wooden object which is the medium of communication with the spirit world, from whence it derives its power. Although there are different types of *ofo*, some of them personal and others institutional, it is the lineage *ofo* belonging to the male elder of the primary family in each community which has far-reaching implications for the traditional Igbo. When leaders gather to discuss serious matters, each brings his lineage *ofo*, which he strikes on the ground to ratify agreements. This act invokes divine sanction on any individual who defies the order, making the *ofo* not only the material symbol of the maintenance of law and order but the most effective instrument for mobilising community consciousness. The Igbo often observe that 'gods are the policemen of society'.

Other methods by which traditional Igbo encode and communicate their cherished values include a variety of oral rituals like prayers, name-giving ceremonies and wise sayings. Repetition, a typical feature of cultures with no developed literary tradition, is central to the Igbo preservation of key values in successive generations.

Naming ceremonies are particularly important in Igbo culture, with lineage elders having the prerogative of choosing personal names for children born in the community. These invariably contain references to the social harmony theme: *Azuka-ego* means 'kin are worth much more than money'; *Adinigwe* and *Odigwe* mean 'it is better to be many'; *Somaadina* translates as 'let me not exist alone'; *Madubunjala* means 'man makes a country wicked'.

While this chapter began by focusing on the moral complexities which lie behind the religious ceremonies of Africa, it has gravitated towards mythological explanations of why Africans hold their beliefs. This is because in Africa's oral tradition myth merges with history and fact to the extent that they are often inextricable. Says Benjamin Ray:

> It is important to see how African myth-history as a whole gives meaning to the world: how the sacred and true events of the past serve to represent the world as it ultimately is, and how these same events may serve as ritual archetypes for the renewal of the natural and human order.

Twelve A

Bewitched, Bothered and Bewildered

Ordinary people living under stress everywhere resort to some form of magic as part of their coping philosophies. A random mixture of common sense, prescription drugs and mystical thought usually does it for westerners, enabling them to struggle through bad times without recourse to murder and mayhem.

Indeed, if the western wonder antidepressant drug Prozac were available to Africans beset by poverty and its attendant ills, it would be welcomed as veritable magic by those with no knowledge of science. Our own ancestors, if unlucky enough to have endured shock treatment as the antidote to depression, might well regard Prozac as a magical substance, too.

While many Africans temper faith with scepticism, most

remain incurably mystical. That is a fact of their nature and experience in particular, and of human nature in general.

Yet we continue to ask, as did the famous anthropologist who led the study of African religion, Professor E Evans-Pritchard: Why does common sense not triumph over superstition? It is a good question, albeit one without an easy answer.

Some years ago, a young English schoolmaster named Allan Smith arrived at a remote village school near Gweru in Zimbabwe. Feeling out of place with no knowledge of the local language or culture, the Voluntary Services Overseas (VSO) teacher seized the first opportunity to participate in a conversation with his African colleagues over tea in the staff room.

They were heatedly discussing a recent witchcraft incident – some of them challenging the imagery of witches riding naked on hyenas at night and some endorsing it – when Allan Smith told them: 'In my country, we used to have women who wore long black dresses with tall black hats and rode on broomsticks at night.' There was a long silence, until one of the teachers who believed in African witches declared scornfully: 'That's stupid!'

Apart from the irony of one superstitious person scoffing at another's supernatural belief, this anecdote raises the comparative question of witch beliefs in England (albeit a long time ago) and those persisting in modern Africa.

The fascinating fact about witchcraft cases in England circa 1700 is that the social environment in which the superstition flourished back then was virtually identical to the conditions prevailing in rural Africa today.

Prior to the technological advances of modern England, belief in witchcraft served as a way of accounting for inexplicable misfortune, just as it does in many African communities. Witchcraft took the blame for most private disasters, to the miscellaneous extent that one group of witches in Maidstone, Kent were charged with the deaths of nine children, two adults, the loss of cattle valued at five hundred pounds, and the shipwreck of a corn cargo.

With no contemporary explanation for the sudden deaths today ascribed to cancer or heart failure, and no germ theory to account for sudden illness, England's forebears believed in supernatural causes. Roger Boyden, for example, was threshing corn one day in 1605 when he was 'suddenly stricken down to the ground and taken lame, both in his right arm and left leg, and so continued till his death', while his daughter Lucy, 'after a ravenous manner did devour an extraordinary proportion of sustenance, yet she pined away to skin and bones and so died'. Margaret Cotton, a neighbour of the Boydens, was subsequently accused of having caused both deaths by witchcraft.

In addition to meeting emotional needs arising from death and personal disaster, witchcraft accusations in England often provided an acceptable explanation for personal disappointment, such as examination failure or sexual impotence. The Elizabethan vicar of Benchley in Kent, for example, blamed the sorcery of one of his parishioners when he kept losing his voice at the pulpit. When Henry VIII grew tired of Anne Boleyn, he claimed he had been attracted to her only because she had seduced him through witchcraft.

While such selfish motives – as when Joan Peterson was executed for witchcraft in 1652 to prevent her implicating others in a conspiracy case – might be parasitic to witch beliefs because they are disingenuous, settling private scores nevertheless fuelled the superstition in England in the same way as fraudulent accusations help perpetuate African witchcraft today.

One of the key psychological reasons for supernatural beliefs in England, as in Africa, was that they offered a means of personal redress in an age when chance was unknown as an explanation for misfortune. King James I described witchcraft accusation as 'a salutary sacrifice for the patient'. Desperate individuals who had endured bad luck over years often grasped witchcraft as the explanation that could also provide a solution. A naval man named William Godfrey, for example, described in 1662 how he had been court-martialled and cashiered; survived poisoning by a ship's surgeon and numerous other life-threatening disasters at sea; then returned home to be arrested for debt. He consequently believed he had been bewitched and wanted the culprit identified by a diviner.

Witch-seekers like William Godfrey usually had a suspect in mind, invariably a neighbour. As is true in Africa, the accused witch in England did not strike from a distance against strangers but already had a vexed relationship with her victim before practising her malice.

The English witch's identity was revealed either by the victim remembering a threat made by a neighbour, or through the utterances of a person in a trance – a possessed individual. In 1653, a small boy in Benenden, Kent, began to have nightmares during which he cried out, 'Father! Father! Here comes a black hairy thing will tease and kill me.' When he was taken to a diviner and added, 'Bess Wood . . . she will kill me' his parents knew that he had been bewitched by a woman already suspected of witchcraft in the village, who had recently quarrelled with the child's mother. Possessed individuals, whether spontaneously citing a suspect or responding to coaxing by a diviner, could usually be relied upon to name a witch.

In England, no less than in Africa, belief in witchcraft obviously relied on a parallel acceptance of traditional healers and magic. The victim of misfortune sought the aid of a diviner in formulating an accusation, and a self-fulfilling prophecy ensued.

It was in the diviner's interests to identify a suspect because he or she had a near-monopoly of witchcraft remedies, and made a living by dispensing them. Since the diviner's reputation relied on a diagnosis plausible to the victim, confirmation of the suspicions already present in the client's mind produced the best results. A mother who asked a mid-seventeenth-century diviner to identify the cause of her child's illness was told, 'Your mistress knows as well who hath wronged her child as I.' In this way, says an observer comparing English and African witchcraft accusations, diviners were 'merely the mouthpiece of corporate hostility towards the suspected witch'. Says English historian Keith Thomas in *Religion and the Decline of Magic*: 'From the initial accusation to the final judicial hearing, the procedure followed in the witch cases reminds us at every stage that men seldom seek a high degree of proof for what they already believe to be true.'

The most common social situation for witchcraft accusation in England arose from a victim being guilty of a breach of neighbourliness by turning from the door an old person – often a childless widow, the most vulnerable member of society – who had come to beg for food or help. Historian Thomas Ady described the uncharitable householder's typical guilty conscience following a subsequent misfortune:

> Presently he cryeth out of some poor innocent neighbour that he or she hath bewitched him. For, saith he, such an old man or woman came lately to my door and desired some relief, and I denied it, and, God forgive me, my heart did rise against her . . . and presently my child, my wife, myself, my horse, my cow, my sheep, my sow, my hog, my dog, my cat, or somewhat, was thus and thus handled in such a strange manner, as I dare swear she

is a witch, or else how should these things be?

Paradoxically, the process of accusation in Ady's anecdote began with the witch – not the victim – being morally wronged, a situation confirmed in most fully documented English witch trials. In this way, the societal function of supernatural beliefs was to reinforce moral standards by postulating that uncharitable behaviour caused repercussions in the natural order. Professor E Evans-Pritchard has written of the Azande in Africa: 'Witch beliefs, like the belief in divine providence, was a manifestation of the same assumption that the likely cause of material misfortune was to be found in some breach of moral behaviour.'

As a theory of causation encompassing a theory of morals, witchcraft is at work even in today's developed world, especially in the United States of America. This is evident in the 'Satanic Panic' of the 1980s, when thousands of cults were believed to be conducting Satanic rituals throughout America, involving the sacrificial mutilation of animals and the sexual abuse of children. Similar cases were subsequently reported in Britain until 1994, when the country's Ministry of Health conducted a study that found no independent corroboration for eyewitness claims of Satanic child abuse.

Another contemporary western parallel to medieval witchcraft is a recent craze practised by psychotherapists – the recovered memory movement. Through suggestive questioning, hypnosis and age-regression, as well as dream interpretation and other psychotherapy techniques, memories of childhood sexual abuse are supposedly recovered from victims who have repressed them for many years. The result – estimated by critics of the movement as well as its proponents – is that over one million people have recovered memories of sexual abuse since 1988, most of which have resulted in irreparable damage to family relationships.

Investigative writer Richard Webster has traced the origins

of the recovered memory movement to a group of American psychotherapists who were so impressed by Judith Herman's acclaimed book *Father-Daughter Incest*, published in 1981, that they decided to set up therapy groups for incest victims in and around Boston. Although these sessions began with women who had never forgotten their sexual abuse, it soon spread and became a wider craze driven by the notion that the subconscious could reveal repressed memories which might account for dysfunctional behaviour, attitudes and relationships.

Gradually, says Webster, memory recovery became memory reconstruction:

> In their pursuit of the hidden memories which supposedly accounted for the symptoms of these women, therapists sometimes used a form of time-limited group therapy. At the beginning of the ten or twelve weekly sessions, patients would be encouraged to set themselves goals. For many patients without memories of incest the goal was to recover such memories. Some of them actually defined their goals by saying, 'I just want to be in the group and feel I belong.' After the fifth session the therapist would remind the group that they had reached the middle of their therapy, with the clear implication that time was running out. As pressure was increased in this way women with no memories would often begin to see images of sexual abuse involving father or other adults, and these images would then be construed as memories or 'flashbacks'.

As more and more patients in America made their accusations, the media seized the subject as an epidemic of child sexual abuse. Says Michael Shermer in *Why People Believe Weird Things*:

> The movement became a full-blown witch craze when Ellen Bass and Laura Davis published *The Courage to Heal: A Guide for Women Survivors of Child Sexual Abuse* in 1988. One of its

conclusions was 'If you think you were abused and your life shows the symptoms, then you were.' The book sold more than 750 000 copies and triggered a recovered memory industry that involved dozens of similar books, talk-show programmes, and magazine and newspaper stories.

Fathers, uncles and family friends in the United States were convicted and imprisoned on the strength of recovered memories. But in 1993, Laura Pasley recanted her recovered childhood memory of sexual abuse, suing her therapist for damages and winning an undisclosed out-of-court settlement. Gary Ramona, father of another recovered memory victim, won his case the following year against the two therapists who had helped his daughter 'remember' him forcing her to perform oral sex on the family dog.

As the number of successful legal appeals mounted, the epidemic of accusations began to lose its impetus, leaving many observers wondering how much damage had been done to the credibility of the genuine victims of child sexual abuse in their quest to bring a real scourge to the attention of society.

Recovered memory accusations mirror the psychology that gave rise to witchcraft in medieval Europe and continues to promote witch beliefs in Africa. Supernatural explanations come not only from a lack of scientific education but from a way of looking at the complexities of life. Believing in things that make us feel better is a natural human response to suffering and bewilderment. Good and bad events happen seemingly randomly to good as well as bad people, unless one finds a scapegoat for misfortune and failure. Science seems to offer only cold logic in its explanation, whereas magic and religion give consoling moral reasons as well as visible or invisible redress.

A Gallup poll published in the *Wall Street Journal* in 1996 showed that 96 per cent of American adults believed in God, 90 per cent in heaven, 79 per cent in miracles and 72 per cent in angels. (Many of those who claimed to be atheists might well change their minds if questioned again during serious illness or old age.) Says Michael Shermer:

> Sceptics, atheists, and militant antireligionists, in their attempts to undermine belief in a higher power, life after death, and divine providence, are butting up against ten thousand years of history and possibly one hundred thousand years of evolution (if religion and belief in God have a biological basis, which some anthropologists believe they do). Throughout all of recorded history, everywhere on the globe, such beliefs and similar percentages are common. Until a secular substitute surfaces, these figures are unlikely to change significantly.

A famous anthropologist, Bronislaw Malinowski, defined the difference between secular and supernatural: 'Science is founded on the conviction that experience, effort, and reason are valid; magic on the belief that hope cannot fail nor desire deceive.'

These definitions merge in the minds and hearts of most people in the world today. Even among professional scientists, many proclaim a secular faith while still believing in an invisible intelligence. Albert Einstein made frequent reference to a higher power, God being his symbol for the mystery of the universe and for the source of awe; a code name for something enigmatic at the core of human existence, which he described as 'something we cannot penetrate'. He often pointed out that scientific equations would never expose that mystery.

Says journalist Dennis Overbye in the *New York Times*:

> Written on a blackboard or a T-shirt, the so-called theory of everything would just lie there waiting for something else to breathe

> life into it and the universe. It would not tell us what we really want to know: Does God love us? Do our lives have any meaning? Nor would it even tell us that science itself has any value. The idea that the universe makes sense, of course, is the sheerest faith of all. The most incomprehensible thing about the universe is that it is comprehensible, Einstein remarked.

In much of Africa, science remains incomprehensible and supernatural beliefs flourish. Many studies have groped to fathom how long it will take Africa to shed these beliefs. It is an important question, not least because fear of the supernatural among city migrants is thought to impact adversely on work stability and therefore on the alleviation of poverty. The underlying assumption of these studies is that the rationale of modern-world development is secular, yet there is much to question in this premise. The western world – where New Age beliefs abound at the start of the twenty-first century – is dependent on scientifically driven technology but is not as committed to a secular rationale, nor as distant from the African belief system, as is generally assumed.

Bibliography

Aschwanden, Herbert (1989). *Karanga Mythology*, Mambo Press, Harare.

Aschwanden, Herbert (1982). *Symbols of Life*, Mambo Press, Harare.

Bacher, Hubert (1980). *Spirits and Power: An Analysis of Shona Cosmology,* Oxford University Press, Cape Town.

Balandier, George (1970). *The Sociology of Black Africa*, André Deutsch Limited.

Bass, Ellen & Davis, Laura (1994). *The Courage to Heal: A Guide for Women Survivors of Child Sexual Abuse,* Harper-Perennial.

Bourdillon, M F C (1993). *Where Are The Ancestors?* University of Zimbabwe.

David, Jay & Harrigton, Helise (1971). *Growing Up African*, William Morrow and Company Incorporated, New York.

Davidson, Basil (1969). *The Africans*, Longmans, Green and Company Limited.

Debrunner, H (1961). *Witchcraft in Ghana*, Presbyterian Book Depot Limited, Accra.

Deng, Francis (1978). *Africans of Two Worlds*, New Haven.

Douglas, Mary (1975). *Implicit Meanings: Essays in Anthropology,* Routledge and Kegan Paul, London.
Ejizu, Christopher I (1986). *Igbo Ritual Symbol, Enugu,* Fourth Dimension Publishers Ltd.
Evans-Pritchard, E E (1937). *Witchcraft, Oracles and Magic among the Azande,* Oxford University Press, London.
Fortes, Meyer (1965). *African Systems of Thought*, Oxford University Press.
Fortes, Meyer & Patterson, Sheila (1975). *Studies in African Social Anthropology*, Academic Press, New York.
Gelfand, Michael (1959). *Shona Ritual,* Juta, Cape Town.
Gelfand, Michael (1967). *The African Witch,* E and S Livingstone Limited, Edinburgh and London.
Gelfand, Michael (1967). *Witchcraft and Sorcery in Rhodesia,* Oxford University Press, London.
Guevara, Che (1969). *Selected Works of Ernesto Guevara,* MIT Press, Cambridge, Mass.
Gulliver, P H (1963). *Social Control in an African Society,* Routledge and Kegan Paul, London.
Haar, Gerrie ter (1992). *Spirit of Africa: the healing ministry of Archbishop Milingo of Zambia,* Hurst, London.
Hammond-Tooke, David (1974). *The Bantu-speaking Peoples of Southern Africa,* Routledge and Paul, London.
Hammond-Tooke, David (1981). *Boundaries and Belief,* Witwatersrand University Press, Johannesburg.
Herman, Judith Lewis (1981). *Father-Daughter Incest,* Harvard University Press.
Idowu, E B (1973). *African Traditional Religion: A Definition,* SCM Press Ltd, London.
King, Noel Q (1970). *Religions of Africa,* Harper and Row, New York.
Lan, David (1985). *Guns and Rain: Guerrillas and Spirit Mediums in Zimbabwe,* J Currey, London.
Laubscher, B J (1937). *Sex, Custom and Psychopathology,* Routledge.
Laubscher, B J (1963). *Where Mystery Dwells,* Timmins.
Laye, Camara (1955). *The Dark Child,* Collins, London.

Lienhardt, R Godfrey (1961). *Divinity and Experience: The Religion of the Dinka*, Clarendon, Oxford.
Lloyd, Alan (1964). *The Drums of Kumasi*, Longmans, Green and Company Limited.
Malinowski, Bronislaw (1945). *The Dynamics of Culture Change*, Yale University Press.
Martin, David & Johnson, Phyllis (1981). *The Struggle for Zimbabwe*, Faber, London.
Martin, Marie-Louise (1975). *Kimbangu: An African Prophet and his Church*, Basil Blackwell, Oxford.
Mbiti, John Samuel (1990). *African Religions and Philosophy*, Heinemann, Oxford.
Mbiti, John Samuel (1970). *Concepts of God in Africa*, SPCK, London.
Milingo, E (1984). *The World in Between: Christian Healing and the Struggle for Spiritual Survival*, C Hurst and Company (Publishers) Limited, London.
Mostert, Noel (1993). *Frontiers: The epic of South Africa's creation and the tragedy of the Xhosa people*, Pimlico, London.
Myatt, Frederick (1966). *The Golden Stool*, William Kimber and Company Limited, London.
Peek, Philip M (1991). *African Divination Systems*, Indiana University Press.
Peires, J B (1989). *The Dead Will Arise*, Ravan Press, Johannesburg.
Pendergrast, Mark (1995). *Victims of Memory: Incest Accusations and Shattered Lives*, Upper Access Books.
Ray, Benjamin C (1976). *African Religions: Symbols, Ritual and Community*, Prentice-Hall Incorporated.
Ranger, Terence (1985). *Peasant Consciousness and Guerrilla War in Zimbabwe*, J Currey, London.
Ranger, Terence (1985). *Soldiers in Zimbabwe's Liberation War*, J Currey, London.
Ranger, Terence (1982). The Death of Chaminuka, *African Affairs*, volume 81.
Radmayne, Alison (1990). *Chikanga: An African Diviner*,

Prentice-Hall, New York.
Sarpong, Peter (1974). *Ghana in Retrospect*, Ghana Publishing Corporation.
Sarpong, Peter (1971). *The Sacred Stools of the Akan*, Accra-tema Ghana.
Scobie, Alistair (1965). *Murder for Magic*, Cassell, London.
Selous, Frederick Courteney (1893). *A Hunter's Wanderings in Africa*, Bentley, London.
Shermer, Michael (1997). *Why People Believe Weird Things*, W H Freeman Company, New York.
Shorter, Alyward (1977). Concepts of Social Justice in Traditional Africa, *Pro Dialogo Bulletin*, 12:32-51.
Skinner, Elliot P (1973). *Peoples and Cultures of Africa*, Natural History Press, New York.
Smith, Edwin W (1950). *African Ideas of God*, Edinburgh House Press, London.
Stapleton, Timothy J (1994). *Maqoma: Xhosa Resistance to Colonial Advance*, J Ball, Johannesburg.
Thomas, Keith (1971). *Religion and the Decline of Magic*, Weidenfeld and Nicholson, London.
Turner, V W (1968): *The Drums of Affliction*, Clarendon Press, Oxford.
Turner, Victor (1967). *The Forest of Symbols*, Cornell University Press, New York.
Uchendu, Victor (1965). *The Igbo of South East Nigeria*, Holt, Rinehart and Winston, New York.
Webster, Richard (1995). *Why Freud Was Wrong*, Basic Books, New York.
Wilson, Monica (1971). *Religion and the Transformation of Society*, Cambridge University Press.

BY THE SAME AUTHOR

Born in Soweto Heidi Holland

Sprawling over fifty square miles, Soweto is the most violent city in the world today. The result of untrammelled urbanisation perverted by apartheid, it is a hostile and forsaken place, even to most of the four million people who call it home.

But Soweto's filthy streets and rickety shacks, representing a painful stage in a difficult transition, are not mere evidence of African decline. They are signs of escape from the hopelessness of a collapsed ethnic system. South Africa's richest optimism is paradoxically embedded in the overcrowded, crime-ravaged hovels of Soweto. They represent the black person's forced choice and willingness to undergo a punishing apprenticeship in a pursuit of a new life.

READ MORE IN PENGUIN

Island in Chains Indres Naidoo – Prisoner 885/63

The Island starts slowly moving back; the reverberations in the boat increase; the engine noise gets louder, and we feel the prison dock being torn from us. We are standing, silent, each at his own porthole, having our last look at what has been our home for ten years.

There is a strange optical effect: the Island seems to get bigger as we get further from it. First we see only the little dock, then the rocks and bushes at either side and, finally, the whole expanding coastline, a complete island; a green and picturesque stretch of land in the ocean, the harsh monotony of its internal life totally hidden by its outer physical beauty . . .

Goodbye, Robben Island, may we never see you again, may all who live on you be liberated, may you go to hell, may you sink into the sea and become part of the bitter memories of the past, of our past, of the past of apartheid.

READ MORE IN PENGUIN

The Aardvark and the Caravan Arthur Goldstuck

Arthur Goldstuck has become synonymous with urban legends in South Africa. In *The Rabbit in the Thorn Tree*, *The Leopard in the Luggage* and *Ink in the Porridge*, he introduced many South Africans for the first time to these stories – intriguing, sometimes bizarre and often hilarious – which continue to do the rounds. Today the term 'urban legend' is routinely used in the mass media as well as in ordinary conversation.

In this omnibus collection, the author has brought many of the most popular urban legends up to date. These are myths, rumours, legends and apocrypha – from the title story of the aardvark and his poetic justice to the fears inspired by technology in the last days of the century, from the car hijackers who never quite get away with it to the politicians who do.